# What is Phonemic Awareness Anyway and WI

Phonemic awareness is the awareness of sounds within words and the ability to isolate, blend, and manipulate these sounds in speech. It's a necessary foundation in learning to read. Phonemic awareness is not an end unto itself. Children need this skill before they can understand the relationship of sounds to print. Marilyn Adams (1990) stated the following as levels of phonemic awareness:

- to hear rhymes and alliteration

- to do oddity tasks (comparing and contrasting the sounds of words for rhyme and alliteration

- to blend and segment syllables

- to segment phonemes

- to manipulate phonemes (adding, deleting, or substituting phonemes and then saying the new word

Many children need no formal instruction to master phonemic awareness skills. However, research shows that about 25% of children lack the ability to acquire phonemic awareness skills without explicit instruction. This book gives teachers and tutors the necessary activities to help their students develop these skills in a fun, yet challenging way.

# How to Use These Activities

This resource is divided into three sections that focus on various levels of phonemic awareness. The first level is beneficial for young students or students whose phonemic awareness skills are at the foundation level. The second level contains more challenging activities, interspersed with easier skills. The last level focuses on manipulation of phonemes and is more complex.

The original idea for this book was based on my efforts to make short, enjoyable phonemic awareness lessons that contained a variety of different activities. The idea grew as I made more and more challenging lessons and shared them with colleagues at Mosier School. We were fortunate to have been a pilot school initiative with the 32° Masonic Learning Centers for Children for four years. During that time 18 teachers were trained in the initial level of Orton-Gillingham instruction and 42 students benefited from the Orton-Gillingham approach. All of the lessons in this book were first tested in our tutoring sessions with great success. Then, adaptations were made for small group and whole classroom instruction.

Each activity begins with a warm-up, where the child is shown three pictures. Student activity sheets are located on the CD provided. There are no words on these student pages as Phonemic awareness is about the sounds of the language, not the letters. The warm-up allows a child to use the pictures to assist in answering questions about the sounds in the words. Students are asked to name the pictures if they can. If they have difficulty, the instructor will give them the correct name and have them repeat each word to make sure they understand the pictures before the activity begins.

There are often slash marks around letters. These slashes mean that the instructor should use the sound versus the name of the letter. For example, if the instruction calls for the student to delete the /k/ in cat, the teacher should make the sound of /k/ rather than say the letter name.

Phonemic awareness instruction need not be arduous. In fact, these activities take about 5-7 minutes and are fun, yet challenging.

There is also mention of Elkonin boxes in many of the lessons. A sample is located on the CD. Students use tokens (buttons, pennies, etc.), pushing one token into each box for each sound of the word given, beginning at the left. For example, for the word cat, the child would push one token for each sound (/k/, /a/, /t/), naming each sound as the token is pushed into the appropriate box.

*Elkonin Box Example*

Within any given activity, you will notice varying amounts of challenge nestled into each section. This is done purposely so that you can pick and choose questions you think your student can handle. It's also done because sometimes more than one child is doing the activity, and there might be a need to vary the challenge. There are also three levels of difficulty within the book, denoted by one star for level one, three stars for level two, and five stars for level three.

## In a Tutoring Environment

Tutors will find these activities perfect for the phonemic portion of any lesson. The activities take about 5-7 minutes if done in entirety. Each lesson begins with a warm-up, where the student looks at pictures and performs various tasks based on them. On the provided CD, there are larger, full color copies of the pictures so that students can have their own to view while the instructor reads the lesson. In the lower levels, there are phoneme or syllable manipulation tasks, and Elkonin boxes are used to help guide the students. Based on the age and ability level of the student, the three levels of tasks can help even older students attempt phonemic manipulation in an enjoyable way.

Within each day's activities, there is enough variety of difficulty so that you can pick and choose how much of the lesson to do depending on the level of the student you are tutoring.

## In a Small Group Environment

The use of these activities in a small guided reading group is a great way to work on improving phonemic skills and have fun at the same time. The large picture card of the day's lesson can be placed on the table in front of the students while the teacher reads the questions. Students can take turns answering questions. The teacher can also control the difficulty of each question based on each student's ability so that all students are successful in the lesson.

## In the General Classroom Environment

In the general classroom, this book is sometimes used as part of a trivia game. The teacher assigns values to the three levels of difficulty in the book. For example, Level One activities are worth 10 points, Level Two activities are worth 20 points, and Level Three Activities are worth 30 points. Students choose questions based on difficulty, and the teacher can assign point amounts depending on what level of question is chosen. The class is usually divided into two teams. Because each lesson has varying degrees of difficulty within it, the teacher has the luxury of choosing a question that suits the child's developmental level in phonemic awareness.

## What Games Can We Play With These Activities?

There are many things you can do to make these activities more game-oriented. The first idea is to use the game boards that are provided in the on the CD. These templates come from the Microsoft Office Site. You can customize them for your students with clipart. A few samples I made are included. When playing a board game I often have the children choose between an easy, challenging, or very hard question. If they answer correctly, they move one, two, or three spaces based on the challenge. Rolling a die can also determine distance traveled.

You can also use inexpensive nerf games from a toy store. Using a nerf basketball hoop, the child shoots after he or she has answered three questions correctly. I do the same with small nets and sticks for our hockey game. Kids are so busy having fun playing the game, they don't realize they're improving their skills! Another popular game is baseball. I draw a baseball diamond on a dry erase board and gather some tokens. The child must answer a question correctly before he or she can move to first, second, third, etc. We keep track of the score, and an incorrect answer is an out. This is a great game to play with groups.

The Hamburger is another great game that you can download from the jc-schools website (www.jc.schools.com). There are pictures of all necessary layers of a hamburger. As each child answers a question correctly, he or she is given one piece of the hamburger. When all the questions have been answered, the student will have the pieces necessary to assemble the hamburger.

Good luck in the implementation of these activities into your tutorial, small group, or classroom setting.

Sandra Donah

October 2008

# Level One Activities

# Activity One*

Warm-up

**Directions: Show the student the following three pictures.**

Ask: Look at the pictures. (wing, book, king)
-Which two words rhyme? (wing, king)
-Where do you hear the /k/ sound in *book* and *king*?
-Give another word that rhymes with *wing* and *king*.

Use Elkonin boxes and have the student do the following:
    -Use the chips to show the sounds in the word *book*. (3)
    -Change the /b/ in *book* to /l/. (look)
    -Change the /oo/ in *look* to /i/. (lick)
    -Add /s/ to the beginning of *lick*. (slick)

Part II

**Word Counting**
How many words do you hear in each sentence? Use your fingers to count the words:
Ben went to the store. (5)
The clock was on the mantel. (6)
John rode the bus to school. (6)
Sunny days will be here soon. (6)
The doctor gave Mary a shot. (6)

**Syllable Counting**
Use Elkonin boxes to count how many syllables are in the following words:
*cleaner* (2)
*flower shop* (3)
*backpack* (2)
*membership* (3)

# Activity Two*

Warm-up

**Directions: Show the student the following three pictures.**

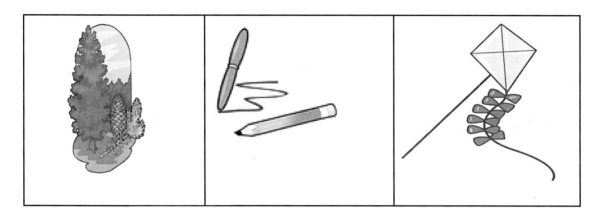

Ask: Look at the pictures. (pine, line, kite)
-Which two words rhyme? (line, pine)
-What vowel sound do you hear in all three words? (/ī/)
-Give two words that rhyme with *kite*.

Use Elkonin boxes and have the student do the following:
       -Use the chips to show the sounds in the word *pine*. (3)
       -Change the /p/ in *pine* to /f/. What's your new word? (fine)
       -Add /d/ to the end of *fine*. (find)
       -Change the /f/ in *find* to /m/. What's your new word? (mind)

Part II

**Syllable Deletion**
Say *notion* without *shun*. (no)
Say *Monday* without *mun*. (day)
Say *climax* without *klī*. (max)
Say *pretend* without *pre*. (tend)
Say *tripod* without *pod*. (try)

**Syllable Addition**
Add *re* to the beginning of *gent*. (regent)
Add *nap* to the beginning of *kin*. (napkin)
Add *pill* to the beginning of *box*. (pillbox)
Add *star* to the beginning of *fish*. (starfish)
Add *place* to the beginning of *ment*. (placement)
Add *con* to the beginning of *fine*. (confine)

# Activity Three *

Warm-up

**Directions: Show the student the following three pictures.**

Ask: Look at the pictures. (anthill, glue, art)
-How many syllables are in each word? (2, 1, 1)
-Say *anthill* without the hill. (ant)
-Give a word that rhymes with *glue*.

Use Elkonin boxes and have the student do the following:
    -Use the chips to show the sounds in *art*. (2)
    -Add /m/ to the beginning of *art*. (mart)
    -Change the /t/ in *mart* to /k/. (mark)
    -Add /s/ to the end of *mark*. (marks)
    -Add *man* to the end of *marks*. (marksman)

Part II

**Rhyme Identification**
Ask: Do these words rhyme?
coat   goat   (y)
frog   cloud  (n)
top    lap    (n)
sink   rink   (y)
plate  rake   (n)
rose   hose   (y)

**Syllable Reversal (Use Elkonin boxes if necessary.)**
Reverse the syllables in *blackout*.   (outblack)
Reverse the syllables in *doorbell*.   (belldoor)
Reverse the syllables in *homeless*.  (lesshome)

# Activity Four*

Warm-up

**Directions: Show the student the following three pictures.**

Ask: Look at the pictures. (pill, kick, spill)
-What vowel sound do you hear in all three words? (/ĭ/)
-What two words rhyme? (pill, spill)
-Give a word that rhymes with *kick*.

Use Elkonin boxes and have the student do the following:
    -Use the chips to show the sounds in *pill*. (3)
    -Delete the first sound. What's left? (ill)
    -Change the /ĭ/ in *ill* to /ŏ/. (all)
    -Now add /b/ to the beginning of *all*. (ball)
    -Add *foot* to the beginning of *ball*. (football)

Part II

**Sound Substitution**
Say *tell*. Change the /t/ in *tell* to /b/. (bell)
Say *pole*. Change the /l/ in *pole* to /k/. (poke)
Say *tribe*. Change the /t/ in *tribe* to /b/. (bribe)
Say *hair*. Change the /h/ in *hair* to /ch/. (chair)
Say *waste*. Change the /w/ in *waste* to /p/. (paste)

**Rhyme Recognition**
Say: What word doesn't rhyme with_____?
| | | | | |
|---|---|---|---|---|
| scale? | pale | male | card | (card) |
| leech? | hunch | beach | reach | (hunch) |
| navy? | wavy | store | gravy | (store) |
| age? | stage | wage | like | (like) |

# Activity Five*

Warm-up

**Directions: Show the student the following three pictures.**

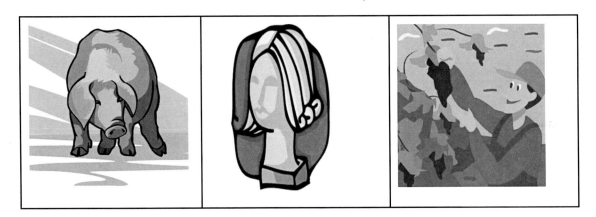

Ask: Look at the pictures. (pig, wig, vine)
-Which two words rhyme? (pig, wig)
-How many sounds are in each of these words? (3)
-Give a word that rhymes with *vine*.

Use Elkonin boxes and have the student do the following:
    -Use the chips to show the sounds in *vine*. (3)
    -Change the first sound in *vine* to /w/. (wine)
    -Add a /d/ to the end of *wine*. (wind)
    -Change the /w/ in *wind* to /b/. (bind)
    -Add /er/ to the end of *bind*. (binder)

Part II

**Sound Isolation**
What sound do you hear in *tower* that's missing in *our*? (/t/)
What sound do you hear in *pout* that's missing in *out*? (/p/)
What sound do you hear in *tame* that's missing in *aim*? (/t/)
What sound do you hear in *box* that's missing in *ox*? (/b/)
What sound do you hear in *steak* that's missing in *take*? (/s/)

**Syllable Counting**
How many syllables do you hear in _____?
traffic? (2)
framework? (2)
trampoline? (3)

# Activity Six*

Warm-up

**Directions: Show the student the following three pictures.**

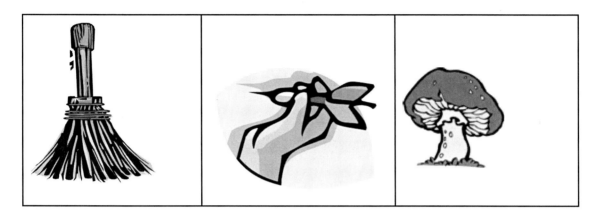

Ask: Look at the pictures. (broom, dart, mushroom)
-Which two words rhyme? (broom, mushroom)
-How many syllables are in *mushroom*? (2)
-Say *mushroom* without the *mush*. (room)
-Give a word that rhymes with *broom*.

Use Elkonin boxes and have the student do the following:
    -Use the chips to show the sounds in *dart*. (3)
    -Delete the first sound in *dart*. (art)
    -Change the /t/ in *art* to /k/. (ark)
    -Add /p/ to the beginning of *ark*. (park)

Part II

## Rhyme Identification
Which word rhymes with _____?

| | | | | |
|---|---|---|---|---|
| ice? | race | rice | bat | (rice) |
| heap? | hit | rap | leap | (leap) |
| glint? | hint | bent | was | (hint) |
| goal? | go | groan | hole | (hole) |
| wish? | dish | went | dump | (dish) |

## Syllable Substitution
Say_____. Instead of _____ say_____.

| | | | |
|---|---|---|---|
| landmark | mark | fill | (landfill) |
| dishpan | pan | towel | (dishtowel) |
| pocket | pock | mark | (market) |

11

# Activity Seven*

Warm-up

**Directions: Show the student the following three pictures.**

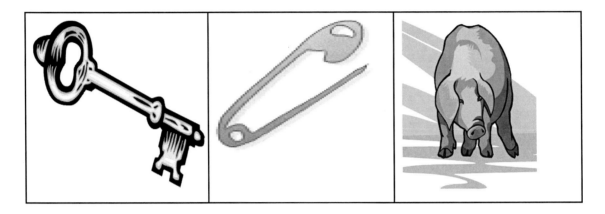

Ask: Look at the pictures. (key, pin, pig)
-Which pictures begin with the same sound? (pin, pig-/p/)
-Is the vowel sound the same in *pig* and *pin*? (yes) What is it? (/ĭ/)
-Give two words that rhyme with *pin*.

Use Elkonin boxes and have the student do the following:
    -Use the chips to show the sounds in *key*. (2)
    -Add /p/ to the end of *key*. (keep)
    -Add *sake* to the beginning of *keep*. (sakekeep)
    -Now switch the syllables. (keepsake)

Part II

**Sound Isolation**
-What sound do you hear in *window* that's not in *wind*? (/ō/)
-What sound do you hear in *time* that's not in *tie*? (/m/)
-What sound do you hear in *brown* that's not in *brow* (/n/)
-What sound do you hear in *paint* that's not in *pain*? (/t/)
-What sound do you hear in *steak* that's not in in *stay*? (/k/)

**Phoneme Substitution**
Say _____. Change the ____ to _____.

| | | | |
|---|---|---|---|
| least | /l/ | /f/ | (feast) |
| mast | /m/ | /p/ | (past) |
| nylon | /n/ | /p/ | (pylon) |
| notch | /n/ | /b/ | (botch) |
| rest | /r/ | /t/ | (test) |

# Activity Eight*

Warm-up

**Directions: Show the student the following three pictures.**

Ask: Look at the pictures. (sink, cat, start)
-What two words have the same beginning sound? (sink, start)
-What two words have the same ending sound? (cat, start)
-Which word begins with a blend? (start-/st/)
-Give a word that rhymes with *sink*.

Use Elkonin boxes and have the student do the following:
    -Use chips to show the sounds in *cat*. (3)
    -Change the /t/ in *cat* to /p/. (cap)
    -Add *baseball* to the beginning of *cap*. (baseball cap)
    -Now switch the words. (cap baseball)

Part II

**Initial Sound Deletion**
Say *bank* without the /b/. (ank)
Say *lucky* without the /l/. (ucky)
Say *pantry* without the /p/. (antry)
Say *reject* without the /r/. (eject)
Say *small* without the /s/. (mall)
Say *sand* without the /s/. (and)

**Final Sound Deletion**
Say *hint* without the /t/. (hin)
Say *nose* without the /z/. (no)
Say *scrape* without the /p/. (scray)
Say *finger* without the /er/. (fing)
Say *last* without the /t/. (lass)

# Activity Nine*

Warm-up

**Directions: Show the student the following three pictures.**

Ask: Look at the pictures. (blew, treadmill, chew)
-What two words have the same ending sound? (blew, chew)
-How many syllables are in the word *treadmill*? (2)
-Give a word that rhymes with *blew*.

Use Elkonin boxes and have the student do the following:
    -Use chips to show the sounds in *chew*. (2)
    -Add /z/ to the end of *chew*. (choose)
    -Change the /ch/ in *choose* to /l/. (lose)
    -Change the /z/ in *lose* to /t/. (loot)
    -Change the /l/ in *loot* to /sh/. (shoot)
    -Add /er/ to the end of *shoot*. (shooter)

Part II

**Rhyme Identification**
Does *jump* rhyme with *lump*? (y)
Does *pick* rhyme with *nip*? (n)
Does *brother* rhyme with *matter*? (n)
Does *trade* rhyme with *laid*? (y)
Does *beast* rhyme with *feast*? (y)

**Segmenting Initial Sounds in Words**
What's the first sound in *taxi*? (/t/)
What's the first sound in *tank*? (/t/)
What's the first sound in *back*? (/b/)
What's the first sound in *chase*? (/ch/)

# Activity Ten*

Warm-up

**Directions: Show the student the following three pictures.**

Ask: Look at the pictures. (whine, think, stink)
-What two words rhyme? (think, stink)
-Add /er/ to the end of whine. (whiner)
-Give a word that rhymes with *whine*.

Use Elkonin boxes and have the student do the following:
    -Use chips to show the sounds in *whine*. (3)
    -Delete the /n/ in *whine* and say the new word. (why)
    -Add /z/ to the end of *why*. (wise)
    -Change the /z/ in *wise* to /t/. (white)

Part II

**Syllable Reversal**
Add *corn* to the end of *pop*. (popcorn)
Switch the parts and say the new word. (cornpop)
Add *pre* to the end of *school*. (schoolpre)
Switch the parts and say the new word. (preschool)
Add *love* to the end of *puppy*. (puppylove)
Switch the parts and say the new word. (lovepuppy)
Add *rattle* to the end of *snake*. (snakerattle)
Switch the parts and say the new word. (rattlesnake)

**Sound Isolation**
Does *corn* end with /n/ or /g/? (/n/)
Does *start* end with /k/ or /t/? (/t/)
Does *jump* end with /m/ or /p/? (/p/)
Does *trapeze* end with /z/ or /s/? (/z/)
Does *rainbow* end with /ō/ or /b/? (/ō/)

# Activity Eleven*

Warm-up

**Directions: Show the student the following three pictures.**

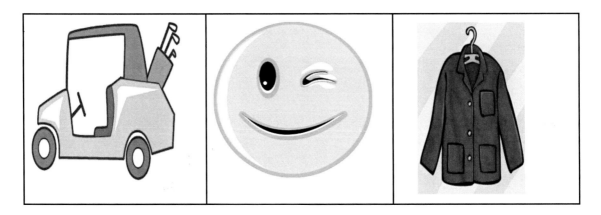

Ask: Look at the pictures. (cart, wink, jacket)
-Which word has more than one syllable. (jacket-2)
-Which two words end with the same sound? (cart, jacket)
-Say *jacket* without the *et*. (jack)
-Give a word that rhymes with *wink*.

Use Elkonin boxes and have the student do the following:
    -Use chips to show the sounds in *cart*. (3)
    -Change the /k/ in *cart* to /m/. (mart)
    -Add /s/ to the beginning of *mart*. (smart)
    -Add *brain* to the beginning of *smart*. (brainsmart)
    -Change *smart* in *brainsmart* to *food*. (brainfood)

Part II

**Segmenting Initial Sounds in Words**
What is the first sound you hear in *table*? (/t/)
What is the first sound you hear in *crab*? (/k/)
What is the first sound you hear in *abdomen*? (/a/)
What is the first sound you hear in *graph*? (/g/)
What is the first sound you hear in *bagel*? (/b/)

**Sound Deletion**
Say *take* without the /t/. (ache)
Say *tie* without the /t/. (ī)
Say *next* without the /t/. (nex)
Say *trap* without the /t/. (rap)
Say *baker* without the /er/. (bake)

# Activity Twelve*

Warm-up

**Directions: Show the student the following three pictures.**

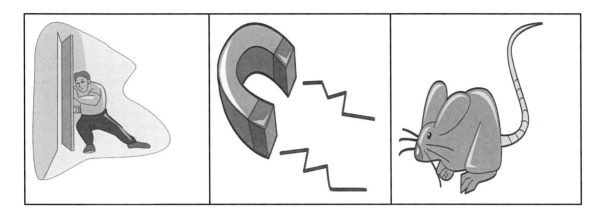

Ask: Look at the pictures. (shut, magnet, mouse)
-What two words have the same ending sound? What is it? (magnet, shut-/t/)
-How many syllables are in the word *magnet*? (2)
-Which word begins with a digraph? (shut-/sh/)
-Give a word that rhymes with *mouse*.

Use Elkonin boxes and have the student do the following:
    -Use chips to show the sounds in *shut*. (3)
    -Change the /sh/ in *shut* to /g/. (gut)
    -Add *er* to the end of *gut*. (gutter)
    -Change the /g/ in *gutter* to /p/. (putter)

Part II

**Syllable Deletion**
Say *number* without *ber*. (num)
Say *sailboat* without *sail*. (boat)
Say *computer* without *er*. (compute)
Say *prairie* without /ē/. (prair)
Say *sentence* without *sen*. (tence)

**Supply Initial Sounds in Words**
What sound do you hear in *sail* that's missing in *ale*? (/s/)
What sound do you hear in *raid* that's missing in *aid*? (/r/)
What sound do you hear in *label* that's missing in *able*? (/l/)
What sound do you hear in *prince* that's missing in *rinse*?(/p/)
What sound do you hear in *goldfish* that's missing in *oldfish*? (/g/)

# Activity Thirteen*

Warm-up

**Directions: Show the student the following three pictures.**

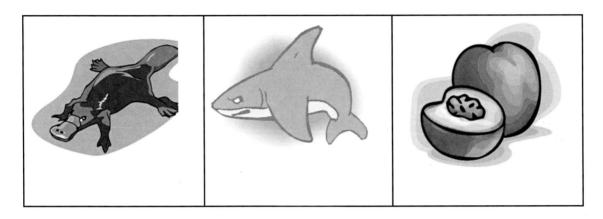

Ask: Look at the pictures. (platypus, shark, peach)
-What two words have the same beginning sound? (platypus, peach-/p/)
-Which words have a digraph in them? (shark-/sh/, peach-/ch/)
-Which word begins with a blend? (platypus-/pl/)
-Add *tree* to the end of *peach*. (peachtree)
-How many syllables do you hear in *platypus*? (3)

Use Elkonin boxes and have the student do the following:
    -Use chips to show the sounds in *peach*. (3)
    -Delete the /p/ in *peach*. (each)
    -Add /r/ to the beginning of *each*. (reach)
    -Change the /ch/ in *reach* to /d/. (read)
    -Add *ing* to the end of *read*. (reading)

Part II

**Rhyme Generation**
Give a word that rhymes with *grand*.
Give a word that rhymes with *lump*.
Give a word that rhymes with *stake*.
Give a word that rhymes with *plot*.
Give a word that rhymes with *track*.

**Segmenting Final Sounds in Words**
What's the last sound in *taxi*? (/ē/)
What's the last sound in *truck*? (/k/)
What's the last sound in *tribe*? (/b/)
What's the last sound in *splice*? (/s/)

# Activity Fourteen*

Warm-up

**Directions: Show the student the following three pictures.**

Ask: Look at the pictures. (skunk, soup, microscope)
-Which two words have the same ending sound? (soup, microscope)
-What blend do you hear at the beginning of *skunk*? (/sk/)
-Give a word that rhymes with *skunk*.
-How many syllables are in *microscope*? (3)

Use Elkonin boxes and have the student do the following:
    -Use chips to show the sounds in *soup*. (3)
    -Change the /s/ in *soup* to /l/. (loop)
    -Add /s/ to the beginning of *loop*. (sloop)
    -Change the /oo/ in *sloop* to /ē/. (sleep)

Part II

**Rhyming Identification**
**Which of these words rhymes with _____?**

| | | | | |
|---|---|---|---|---|
| Fruit | tool | slip | boot | (boot) |
| date: | cave | might | late | (late) |
| gain: | main | soap | doe | (main) |
| back: | draft | pack | light | (pack) |
| pocket: | traffic | rocket | wishing | (rocket) |

**Syllable Reversal**
Reverse the syllables in *drumstick*. (stickdrum)
Reverse the syllables in *housegreen*. (greenhouse)
Reverse the syllables in *cargo*. (gocar)
Reverse the syllables in *plastic*. (ticplas)

# Activity Fifteen*

Warm-up

**Directions: Show the student the following three pictures.**

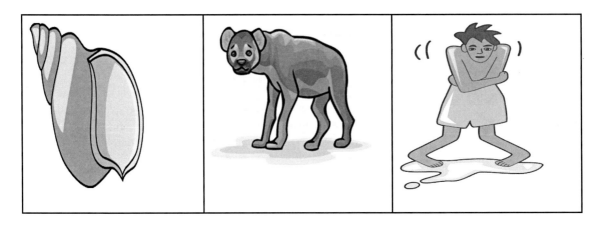

Ask: Look at the pictures. (shell, hyena, shiver)
-What two words have the same beginning sound? (shell, shiver)
-How many syllables are in *hyena*? (3)
-Say *shiver* without *er*. (shiv)
-Change the /ĭ/ in *shiv* to /ŭ/. (shove)
-Give a word that rhymes with *shell*.

Use Elkonin boxes and have the student do the following:
    -Use chips to show the syllables in *shiver*. (2)
    -Delete the /er/ in *shiver*. (shiv)
    -Change the /sh/ in *shiv* to /l/. (live)
    -Add *ing* to the end of *live*. (living)

Part II

**Segmenting Syllables**
Clap out the syllables in *photographer*. (4)
Clap out the syllables in *transport*. (2)
Clap out the syllables in *invitation*. (4)
Clap out the syllables in *pine*. (1)
Clap out the syllables in *lightning*. (2)

**Matching Rhyme**
| | | | | |
|---|---|---|---|---|
| What word rhymes with *clad*? | clam | dad | line | (dad) |
| What word rhymes with *pace*? | lace | make | yes | (lace) |
| What word rhymes with *plant*? | stop | rat | can't | (can't) |
| What word rhymes with *drone*? | paste | lone | long | (lone) |

# Activity Sixteen*

Warm-up

**Directions: Show the student the following three pictures.**

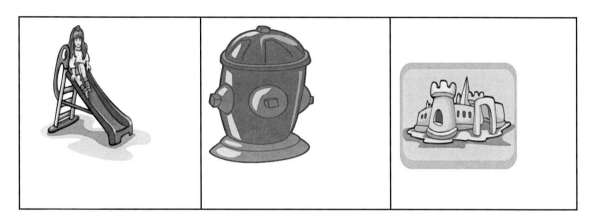

Ask: Look at the pictures. (slide, hydrant, moat)
-What two words have the same ending sound? (hydrant, moat-/t/)
-Which word has a blend at the beginning? (slide-/sl/)
-How many syllables are in each word? (1, 2, 1)
-Give a word that rhymes with *moat*.

Use Elkonin boxes and have the student do the following:
    -Use chips to show the sounds in *moat*. (3)
    -Delete the /t/ in *moat*. (mow)
    -Change the /ō/ in *mow* to /ī/. (my)
    -Add /t/ to the end of *my*. (might)

Part II

**Syllable Deletion**
Say *stomach* without *ick*. (stom)
Say *ladybug* without *bug*. (lady)
Say *eardrum* without *ear*. (drum)
Say *pineapple* without *pine*. (apple)
Say *cliffhanger* without *er*. (cliffhang)
Say *transcript* without *tran*. (script)

**Substituting Initial Sounds**
Say *paste*. Instead of /p/ say /w/. (waste)
Say *jump*. Instead of /j/ say /l/. (lump)
Say *chair*. Instead of /ch/ say /b/. (bear)
Say *tank*. Instead of /t/ say /th/. (thank)
Say *cape*. Instead of /k/, say /t/. (tape)

# Activity Seventeen*

Warm-up

**Directions: Show the student the following three pictures.**

Ask: Look at the pictures. (popcorn, spaghetti, goat)
-What word has the most syllables in it? (spaghetti-3)
-Say *popcorn* backwards. (cornpop)
-Which word ends with a vowel sound? What is it? (spaghetti-/ē/)
-Give a word that rhymes with *goat*.

Use Elkonin boxes and have the student do the following:
    -Use chips to show the sounds in *goat*. (3)
    -Delete the /t/ in *goat*. (go)
    -Add /l/ to *go*. (goal)
    -Change the /g/ in *goal* to /m/. (mole)
    -Add *hole* to the end of *mole*. (molehole)

Part II

**Rhyme Identification**
Does *tattle* rhyme with *rattle*? (y)
Does *stone* rhyme with *rope*? (n)
Does *blackened* rhyme with *pickle*? (n)
Does *stove* rhyme with *drove*? (y)
Does *rash* rhyme with *hush*? (n)

**Segmenting Initial Sounds in Words**
What's the first sound in *temple*? (/t/)
What's the first sound in *trade*? (/t/)
What's the first sound in *baby*? (/b/)
What's the first sound in *strap*? (/s/)

# Activity Eighteen*

Warm-up

**Directions: Show the student the following three pictures.**

Ask: Look at the pictures. (kayak, koala, shed)
-What two words have the same beginning sound? (kayak, koala-/k/)
-How many syllables are there in *koala*? (3)
-What digraph do you hear at the beginning of *shed*? (/sh/)
-Give a word that rhymes with *shed.*

Use Elkonin boxes and have the student do the following:
    -Use chips to show the sounds in *shed*. (3)
    -Delete /sh/ from *shed*. (ed)
    -Add /l/ to the beginning of *ed*. (led)
    -Add /s/ to the beginning of *led*. (sled)
    -Add *bob* to the beginning of *sled*. (bobsled)
    -Reverse the syllables in *bobsled*. (sledbob)

Part II

**Syllable Deleting**
Say *Friday* without *day*. (fry)
Say *polar* without *er*. (pole)
Say *remain* without *re*. (main)
Say *lobster* without *ster*. (lob)
Say *pineapple* without *pine*. (apple)

**Sound Blending**
Tap out the sounds in the word *tape*. (/t/ /ā/ /p/)
Tap out the sounds in the word *mash*. (/m/ /a/ /sh/)
Tap out the sounds in the word *lush*. (/l/ /u/ /sh/)
Tap out the sounds in the word *nose*. (/n/ /ō/ /z/)

# Activity Nineteen*

Warm-up

**Directions: Show the student the following three pictures.**

Ask: Look at the pictures. (glider, match, playpen)
-What two words have the same number of syllables? (glider, playpen-2)
-Say *playpen* backwards. (penplay)
-Say *glider* without the *er*. (glide)
-Which two words have blends in them? (glider-/gl/, playpen-/pl/)
-Give a word that rhymes with *match*.

Use Elkonin boxes and have the student do the following:
    -Use chips to show the sounds in *match*. (3)
    -Delete the /m/ in *match*. (atch)
    -Add /p/ to the beginning of *atch*. (patch)
    -Add *work* to the end of *patch*. (patchwork)
    -Add *quilt* to the end of *patchwork*. (patchwork quilt)

Part II

**Working With Beginning Blends**
Think of a word that begins with the blend /sl/.
Think of a word that begins with the blend /br/.
Think of a word that begins with the blend /sn/.
Think of a word that begins with the blend /cl/.
Think of a word that begins with the blend /tr/.

**Substituting Initial Sounds in Words**
Say *round*. Instead of /r/, say /p/. (pound)
Say *gold*. Instead of /g/, say /f/. (fold)
Say *gopher*. Instead of /g/, say /l/. (loafer)

# Activity Twenty*

Warm-up

**Directions: Show the student the following three pictures.**

Ask: Look at the pictures. (shamrock, castle, dew)
-How many syllables are in each of these words? (2, 2, 1)
-What digraph do you hear at the beginning of *shamrock*? (/sh/)
-Say *shamrock* without *sham*. (rock)
-Say a word that rhymes with *dew*.

Use Elkonin boxes and have the student do the following:
    -Use chips to show the sounds in *dew*. (2)
    -Add /l/ to the end of *dew*. (duel)
    -Change the /oo/ in *duel* to /ī/. (dial)
    -add /d/ to the end of *dial*. (dialed)

Part II

**Segmenting Syllables**
How many syllables are in *hippopotamus*? (5)
How many syllables are in *concentration*? (4)
How many syllables are in *plant*? (1)
How many syllables are in *snowstorm*? (2)
How many syllables are in *ravioli*? (4)

**Syllable Addition**
Add *cliff* to the beginning of *hanger*. (cliffhanger)
Add *freeze* to the beginning of *er*. (freezer)
Add *fire* to the beginning of *place*. (fireplace)
Add *ear* to the beginning of *drum*. (eardrum)
Add *free* to the beginning of *quent*. (frequent)

# Activity Twenty-One*

Warm-up

**Directions: Show the student the following three pictures.**

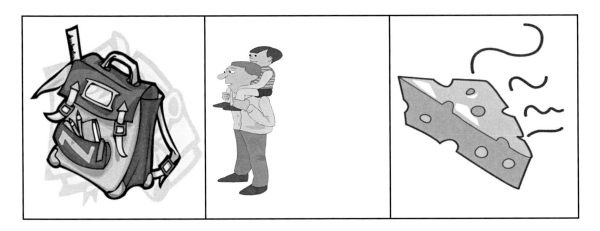

Ask: Look at the pictures. (backpack, piggyback, cheese)
-How many syllables are in each of these words? (2, 3, 1)
-What digraph do you hear at the beginning of *cheese*? (/ch/)
-What syllable is the same in *piggyback* and *backpack*? (back)

Use Elkonin boxes and have the student do the following:
    -Use chips to show the sounds in *cheese*. (3)
    -Delete the /ch/ in *cheese*. (ease)
    -Change the /z/ in *ease* to /t/. (eat)
    -Add /b/ to the beginning of *eat*. (beat)

Part II

**Counting Words**
**How many words do you hear in this sentence?**
John went to the mall. (5)
Sarah likes jumping rope best. (5)
The noisy children went on the ride. (7)
The church is around the corner. (6)
My dog eats pizza. (4)
Flowers smell wonderful. (3)

**Rhyme Generation**
Find a word that rhymes with *plug*.
Find a word that rhymes with *vase*.
Find a word that rhymes with *black*.
Find a word that rhymes with *chip*.

# Activity Twenty-Two*

Warm-up

**Directions: Show the student the following three pictures.**

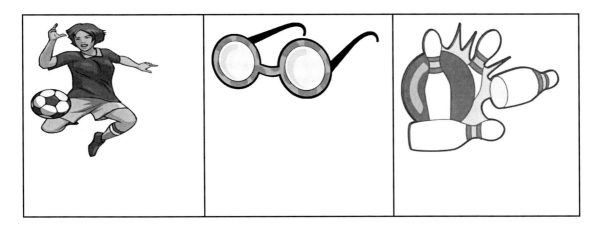

Ask: Look at the pictures. (kick, glasses, strike)
-Which two words have the same ending sound? (kick, strike)
-What blends do you hear at the beginning of *glasses* and *strike*? (/gl/, /str/)
-How many syllables are in *glasses*? (2)
-Find a word that rhymes with *strike*.

Use Elkonin boxes and have the student do the following:
    -Use chips to show the sounds in *kick*. (3)
    -Delete the first sound in *kick*. (ick)
    -Add /t/ to the beginning of *ick*. (tick)
    -Add /s/ to the beginning of *tick*. (stick)

Part II
**Word Reversal**
Switch the words in *homeless*. (lesshome)
Switch the words in *honeybee*. (beehoney)
Switch the words in *meantime*. (time mean)
Switch the words in *manmade*. (mademan)
Switch the words in *knapsack*. (sackknap)
Switch the words in *slingshot*. (shotsling)

**Syllable Addition**
Add *re* to the beginning of *verse*. (reverse)
Add *care* to the beginning of *free*. (carefree)
Add *stu* to the beginning of *dent*. (student)
Add *cole* to the beginning of *gate*. (colgate)

# Activity Twenty-Three*

Warm-up

**Directions: Show the student the following three pictures.**

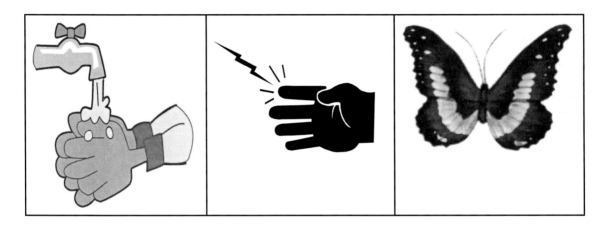

Ask: Look at the pictures. (wash, shock, butterfly)
-What two words have the same digraph in them? (wash, shock)
-Which word has the most syllables? (butterfly-3)
-Reverse the first and last words in *butterfly*. (fly butter)
-Give a word that rhymes with *shock*.

Use Elkonin boxes and have the student do the following:
- Use chips to show the syllables in *butterfly*. (3)
- Delete the last syllable in *butterfly*. (butter)
- Add *cream* to the end of *butter*. (butter cream)
- Change *butter* in *butter cream* to *ice*. (ice cream)

Part II

**Syllable Addition (ending)**
Add *er* to the end of *poke*. (poker)
Add *pier* to the end of /ŭ/. (appear)
Add *stat* to the end of *choo*. (choostat)
Add *time* to the end of *show*. (showtime)
Add *out* to the end of *work*. (workout)

**Identifying Rhyme Oddity**
**Which word does not rhyme with the other three?**
poke   soak   pack   joke   (pack)
try    fine   buy    sigh   (fine)
ball   clip   trip   lip    (ball)
black  tack   lad    jack   (lad)

# Activity Twenty-Four*

Warm-up

**Directions: Show the student the following three pictures.**

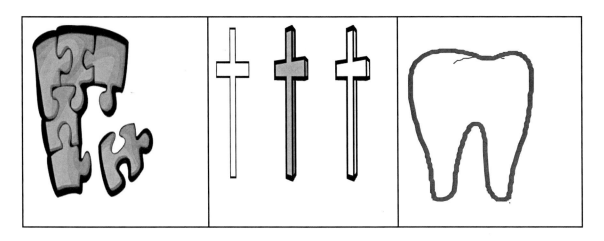

Ask: Look at the pictures. (jigsaw, cross, tooth)
-Which word has a digraph? (tooth)
-What blend do you hear at the beginning of *cross*? (/cr/)
-How many syllables are there in *jigsaw*? (2)
-Say *jigsaw* backwards. (saw jig)
-Say a word that rhymes with *cross*.

Use Elkonin boxes and have the student do the following:
    -Use chips to show the sounds in *tooth*. (3)
      -Delete the /th/ in *tooth*. (too)
      -Add /b/ to the end of *too*. (tube)
      -Add *ing* to the end of *tube*. (tubing)
      -Switch the syllables in *tubing*. (ingtube)

Part II

**Matching Final Sound to Word**
Does *absent* end with a /s/ or /t/? (/t/)
Does *compass* end with a /m/ or a /s/? (/s/)
Does *fabric* end with a /k/ or a /t/? (/k/)
Does *nutmeg* end with a /g/ or a /j/? (/g/)
Does *keyboard* end with a /d/ or a /r/? (/d/)

**Segmenting Initial Sounds in Words**
What's the first sound in *plastic*? (/p/)
What's the first sound in *pencil*? (/p/)
What's the first sound in *contest*? (/k/)

# Activity Twenty-Five*

Warm-up

**Directions: Show the student the following three pictures.**

Ask: Look at the pictures. (scratch, scream, thumb)
-Which two words have the same ending sound? (scream, thumb-/m/)
-What digraph do you hear in *scratch*? (/ch/)
-What digraph can you find at the beginning of *thumb*? (th-thumb)
-Say a word that rhymes with *scream*.

Use Elkonin boxes and have the student do the following:
    -Use chips to show the sounds in *thumb*. (3)
    -Add /p/ to the end of *thumb*. (thump)
    -Change the /th/ in *thump* to /p/. (pump)
    -Add *gas* to the beginning of *pump*. (gas pump)

Part II

**Sound Recognition**
Does *jump* have 3 sounds? (n-4)
Does *trip* have 4 sounds? (y)
Does *paste* have 4 sounds? (y)
Does *splash* have 5 sounds? (y)
Does *lake* have 4 sounds? (n-3)
Does *grape* have 3 sounds? (n-4)

**Word Generation**
Think of a word that ends with /sh/.
Think of a word that ends with /g/.
Think of a word that ends with /k/.
Think of a word that ends with /d/.
Think of a word that ends with /t/.

# Activity Twenty-Six*

Warm-up

**Directions: Show the student the following three pictures.**

Ask: Look at the pictures. (hippopotamus, scrub, horse)
-Which two words have the same ending sound? (hippopotamus, horse-/s/)
-What blend do you hear at the beginning of *scrub*? (/scr/)
-Which word has the most syllables? How many? (hippopotamus-5)
-Give a word that rhymes with *horse*.

Use Elkonin boxes and have the student do the following:
    -Use chips to show the sounds in *horse*. (3)
    -Change the /h/ in *horse* to /f/. (force)
    -Change the /s/ in *force* to /t/. (fort)
    -Delete the /t/ in *fort*. (for)
    -Add *arm* to the end of *for*. (forearm)
    -Change *arm* in forearm to *warn*. (forewarn)

Part II

**Initial Sound Substitution**
Say *very*. Instead of /v/, say /b/. (berry)
Say *mountain*. Instead of /m/, say /f/. (fountain)
Say *wheeze*. Instead of /wh/, say /t/. (tease)
Say *black*. Instead of /b/, say /s/. (slack)
Say *could*. Instead of /k/, say /w/. (would)

**Syllable Deletion**
Say *greyhound* without *hound*. (grey)
Say *backbone* without *bone*. (back)
Say *triplet* without *let*. (trip)

# Activity Twenty-Seven*

Warm-up

**Directions: Show the student the following three pictures.**

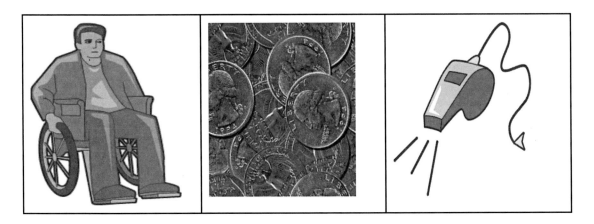

Ask: Look at the pictures. (wheelchair, quarter, whistle)
-Which two words have the same ending sound? (wheelchair, quarter-/r/)
-What digraph do you hear at the beginning of *wheelchair* and *whistle*? (wh)
-How many syllables are in each of these words? (2)
-Say *quarter* backwards. (erquart)

Use Elkonin boxes and have the student do the following:
    -Use chips to show the syllables in *wheelchair*. (2)
    -Delete *chair* In *wheelchair*. (wheel)
    -Use the chips to show the sounds in *wheel*. (3)
    -Change the /l/ in *wheel* to /t/. (wheat)
    -Change the /ē/ in *wheat* to /ī/. (white)
    -Add *house* to the end of *white*. (white house)

Part II

**Rhyme Identification**
Does *our* rhyme with *power*? (y)
Does *grain* rhyme with *gate*? (n)
Does *blast* rhyme with *rust*? (n)
Does *tingle* rhyme with *mingle*? (y)
Does *stagger* rhyme with *stump*? (n)

**Segmenting Initial Sounds in Words**
What's the first sound in *firestorm*? (/f/)
What's the first sound in *gradual*? (/g/)
What's the first sound in *cola*? (/k/)

# Activity Twenty-Eight*

Warm-up

**Directions: Show the student the following three pictures.**

Ask: Look at the pictures. (telephone, turtle, sack)
-Which two words have the same beginning sound? (telephone, turtle-/t/)
-Which word has the most syllables? (telephone-3)
-Say *telephone* without *tele*. (phone)
-Add *call* to the end of *phone*. (phonecall)

Use Elkonin boxes and have the student do the following:
    -Use chips to show the sounds in *sack.* (3)
    -Delete the /k/ in *sack.* (sa)
    -Add /p/ to the end of *sa.* (sap)
    -Change the /s/ in *sap* to /g/. (gap)

Part II

**Rhyme Identification**
Does *blame* rhyme with *tame*? (y)
Does *grain* rhyme with *late*? (n)
Does *brother* rhyme with *mother*? (y)
Does *spoon* rhyme with *moon*? (y)
Does *voice* rhyme with *chase*? (n)
Does *slice* rhyme with *rice*? (y)

**Segmenting Initial Sounds in Words**
What's the first sound in *basket*? (/b/)
What's the first sound in *chomp*? (/ch/)
What's the first sound in *flint*? (/f/)
What's the first sound in *shower*? (/sh/)

# Activity Twenty-Nine*

Warm-up

**Directions: Show the student the following three pictures.**

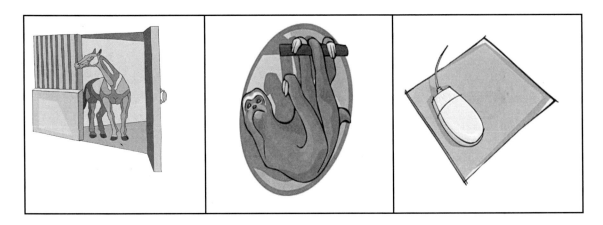

Ask: Look at the pictures. (stall, sloth, mouse pad)
-What two words have the same vowel sound? (stall, sloth-/o/)
-What word has the most syllables? (mousepad)
-Give a word that rhymes with *stall*.
-Say *mousepad* without *mouse*. (pad)

Use Elkonin boxes and have the student do the following:
    -Use chips to show the sounds in *pad*. (3)
    -Change the /d/ in *pad* to /t/. (pat)
    -Add /s/ to the beginning of *pat*. (spat)
    -Change the /a/ in *spat* to /i/. (spit)
    -Add *ball* to the end of *spit*. (spitball)

Part II

**Syllable Substitution**
Say *network*. Instead of *net,* say *home*. (homework)
Say *needlework*. Instead of *needle,* say *paper*. (paperwork)
Say *newspaper*. Instead of *news,* say *colored*. (colored paper)
Say *nightgown*. Instead of *gown,* say *mare*. (nightmare)
Say *outsmart*. Instead of *smart,* say *side*. (outside)

**Segmenting Sounds in Words**
What are the sounds in *play*? (/p/ /l/ /ā/)
What are the sounds in *back*? (/b/ /a/ /ck/)
What are the sounds in *great*? (/g/ /r/ /ā/ /t/)
What are the sounds in *stag*? (/s/ /t/ /a/ /g/)

# Activity Thirty*

Warm-up

**Directions: Show the student the following three pictures.**

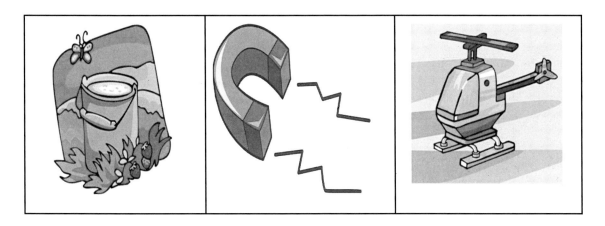

Ask: Look at the pictures. (pail, magnet, helicopter)
-Which word has the most syllables? (helicopter-4)
-Say *helicopter* without the *er*. (helicopt)
-Say *magnet* backwards. (netmag)
-Give a word that rhymes with *pail*.

Use Elkonin boxes and have the student do the following:
    -Use chips to show the sounds in *pail*. (3)
    -Delete the /p/ in *pail*. (ail)
    -Change the /l/ in *ail* to /p/. (ape)
    -Add /sh/ to the beginning of *ape*. (shape)
    -Add /less/ to the end of *shape*. (shapeless)

Part II

**Blending Sounds To Make Words**
What word am I saying as I talk like a robot?
/b/ /r/ /oo/ /m/     (broom)
/ch/ /i/ /l/     (chill)
/b/ /ā/ /s/ /t/     (baste)
/f/ /l/ /ō/     (flow)
/s/ /t/ /r/ /a/ /p/     (strap)

**Segmenting Initial Sounds in Words**
What's the last sound in *baboon*? (/n/)
What's the last sound in *trunk*? (/k/)
What's the last sound in *stove*? (/v/)

# Activity Thirty-One*

Warm-up

**Directions: Show the student the following three pictures.**

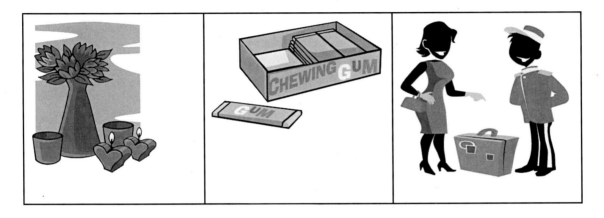

Ask: Look at the pictures. (vase, chewing gum, vacation)
-Which words have the same beginning sound? (vase, vacation-/v/)
-Which words have the same vowel sound? (vase, vacation)
-What word has a digraph in it? (chew-/ch/)
-Give a word that rhymes with *vase*.

Use Elkonin boxes and have the student do the following:
    -Use chips to show the sounds in *veil*. (3)
    -Delete the /v/ in *veil*. (ail)
    -Add /t/ to the beginning of *ail*. (tail)
    -Add /s/ to the beginning of *tail*. (stale)
    -Add *mate* to the end of *stale*. (stalemate)

Part II

**Identifying Hidden Syllables in Words**
Is the word *bone* in the word *hambone*? (y)
-*elbow*? (n)
-*funnybone*? (y)
Is the word *ham* in *hamster*?
-*hambone*? (y)
-*Hampton*? (y)

**Rhyme Oddity**
**Which Word Doesn't Rhyme?**

| stamp | lamp | jump | (jump) |
| rice  | help | yelp | (rice) |

# Activity Thirty-Two*

Warm-up

**Directions: Show the student the following three pictures.**

Ask: Look at the pictures. (fruit, skirt, broom)
-Which two words end with the same sound? (fruit, skirt-/t/)
-Which two words have the same vowel sound? (fruit, broom-oo)
-How many syllables are in each of these words? (1, 1, 1)
-Give a word that rhymes with *broom*.

Use Elkonin boxes and have the student do the following:
    -Use chips to show the sounds in *fruit*. (4)
    -Delete the /f/ in *fruit*. (root)
    -Delete the /t/ in *root*. (roo)
    -Add /m/ to the end of *roo*. (room)
    -Add *mate* to the end of *room*. (roommate)

Part II

**Initial Consonant Identification**
Which word begins with the same first sound you hear in *juice*?
gate        jet        moose        (jet)
Which word begins with the same first sound you hear in *pants*?
bate        stand        pet        (pet)
Which word begins with the same first sound you hear in *gable*?
Grape        table        bent        (grape)

**Syllable Addition**
Add *box* to the end of *flower*. (flowerbox)
Add *it* to the end of *spir*. (spirit)
Add *un* to the beginning of *real*. (unreal)
Add /i-e/ to the beginning of *land*. (island)

# Activity Thirty-Three*

Warm-up

**Directions: Show the student the following three pictures.**

Ask: Look at the pictures. (pickle, banana, pail)
-Which two words end with the same sound? (pickle, pail-/l/)
-Which two words have the same first sound? (pickle, pail)
-How many syllables are in each of these words? (2, 3, 1)
-Give a word that rhymes with *pail*.

Use Elkonin boxes and have the student do the following:
    -Use chips to show the sounds in *pail*. (3)
    -Delete the /p/ in *pail*. (ail)
    -Add /m/ to the beginning of *ail*. (mail)
    -Add *man* to the end of *mail*. (mailman)

Part II

**Syllable Addition**
Add *in* to the beginning of *sist*. (insist)
Add *sales* to the beginning of *man*. (salesman)
Add *try* to the beginning of *pod*. (tripod)
Add *cry* to the beginning of *sis*. (crisis)
Add *toe* to the beginning of *tem*. (totem)
Add *snap* to the beginning of *shot*. (snapshot)

**Syllable Reversal**
Reverse the syllables in *horsefly*. (flyhorse)
Reverse the syllables in *powwow*. (wowpow)
Reverse the syllables in *complex*. (plexcom)
Reverse the syllables in *hairstyle*. (stylehair)

# Activity Thirty-Four*

Warm-up

**Directions: Show the student the following three pictures.**

Ask: Look at the pictures. (pills, glue, jigsaw)
-Which two words have the same vowel sound? (jigsaw, pills-/i/)
-Which word has the most syllables? (jigsaw-2)
-Give a word that rhymes with *glue*.

Use Elkonin boxes and have the student do the following:
    -Use chips to show the sounds in *pill*. (3)
    -Delete the /p/ in *pill*. (ill)
    -Add /r/ to the beginning of *ill*. (rill)
    -Add /g/ to the beginning of *rill*. (grill)
    -Add *barbecue* to the beginning of *grill*. (barbecue grill)

Part II

**Initial Consonant Identification**
Which word begins with the same first sound you hear in *grape*?
tape        goat        stuck        (goat)
Which word begins with the same first sound you hear in *staple*?
sail        rope        fill        (sail)
Which word begins with the same first sound you hear in *Valentine*?
vein        table        bent        (vein)

**Rhyme Generation**
Give two words that rhyme with...
leech
grow

# Activity Thirty-Five*

Warm-up

**Directions: Show the student the following three pictures.**

Ask: Look at the pictures. (manhole, puck, pout)
-What sounds do each of these pictures begin with? (/m/, /p/)
-Which word has the most syllables? (manhole-2)
-Give a word that rhymes with *puck*.
-Reverse the syllables in *manhole*. (holeman)

Use Elkonin boxes and have the student do the following:
    -Use chips to show the sounds in *puck*. (3)
    -Delete the /p/ in *puck*. (uck)
    -Add /l/ to the beginning of *uck*. (luck)
    -Add *pot* to the beginning of *luck*. (potluck)
    -Reverse the syllables in *potluck*. (luckpot)

Part II

**Sound Isolation**
What sound do you hear in *white* that's missing in *why*. (/t/)
What sound do you hear in *keg* that's missing in *egg*. (/k/)
What sound do you hear in *rash* that's missing in *ash*? (/r/)
What sound do you hear in winch that's missing in inch? (/w/)
What sound do you hear in *thin* that's missing in *in*? (/th/)

**Sound Deletion**
Say *milk* without the /k/. (mill)
Say *cork* without the second /k/. (core)
Say *quake* without the /qu/. (ake)
Say *leash* without the /sh/. (Lee)

# Activity Thirty-Six*

Warm-up

**Directions: Show the student the following three pictures.**

Ask: Look at the pictures. (frog, friends, Frankenstein)
-What blend do all three words begin with? (/fr/)
-How many syllables are in each of these words? (1, 1, 3)
-Find a word that rhymes with *frog*.

Use Elkonin boxes and have the student do the following:
    -Use chips to show the sounds in *frog*. (4)
    -Delete the /f/ in *frog*. (rog)
    -Change the /o/ in *rog* to /i/. (rig)
    -Change the /r/ in *rig* to /f/. (fig)
    -Add *meant* to the end of *fig*. (figment)

Part II
**Syllable Reversal**
Reverse the syllables in *mincemeat*. (meatmince)
Reverse the syllables in *standby*. (bystand)
Reverse the syllables in *propel*. (pelpro)
Reverse the syllables in *blindfold*. (foldblind)
Reverse the syllables in *bedroll*. (rollbed)


**Final Consonant Isolation**
Which one of these words has a different ending sound?
| | | | |
|---|---|---|---|
| jump | strap | teach | (teach) |
| stale | brag | hill | (brag) |
| grace | smart | hint | (grace) |
| black | shamrock | giant | (giant) |

# Activity Thirty-Seven*

Warm-up

**Directions: Show the student the following three pictures.**

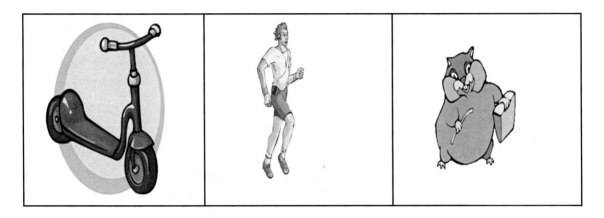

Ask: Look at the pictures. (scooter, jog, hamster)
-Which two words end with the same sound? (hamster, scooter-/r/)
-Say *hamster* backwards. (sterham)
-Say *hamster* without *ster*. (ham)
-Add *bone* to the end of *ham*. (hambone)
-How many syllables are in each of these words? (2, 1, 2)
-Give a word that rhymes with *jog*.

Use Elkonin boxes and have the student do the following:
    -Use chips to show the sounds in *jog*. (3)
    -Delete the /j/ in *jog*. (og)
    -Add /d/ to the beginning of *og*. (dog)
    -Add *house* to the end of *dog*. (doghouse)
    -Reverse the syllables in *doghouse*. (housedog)

Part II

**Initial Sound Identification**
Does *stapler* begin with /t/ or /s/? (/s/)
Does *triceratops* begin with /t/ or /r/? (/t/)
Does *flower* begin with /r/ or /f/? (/f/)
Does *puppy* begin with /p/ or /l/? (/p/)
Does *baker* begin with /k/ or /b/? (/b/)

**Final Sound Identification**
What is the last sound you hear in *manual*? (/l/)
What is the last sound you hear in *handkerchief*? (/f/)
What is the last sound you hear in *strawberry*? (/ē/)

# Activity Thirty-Eight*

Warm-up

**Directions: Show the student the following three pictures.**

Ask: Look at the pictures. (checkerboard, janitor, shell)
-Say checkerboard without board. (checker)
-Reverse the first and last words in *checkerboard*. (boardchecker)
-What two words have the same vowel sound? (checkerboard, shell-/e/)
-How many syllables are in each of these words? (3, 3, 1)
-Give a word that rhymes with *shell*.

Use Elkonin boxes and have the student do the following:
    -Use chips to show the sounds in *shell*. (3)
    -Delete the /sh/ in shell. (el)
    -Add *bow* to end of *el*. (elbow)
    -Reverse the syllables in *elbow*. (bōell)

Part II

**Syllable Deletion**
Say *youthful* without *ful*. (youth)
Say *employ* without *em*. (ploy)
Say *tenderloin* without *loin*. (tender)
Say *pillbox* without *box*. (pill)
Say *python* without *thon*. (pie)

**Word Reversal**
Say *standerby* backwards. (bystander)
Say *pointneedle* backwards. (needlepoint)
Say *letcover* backwards. (coverlet)
Say *tieneck* backwards. (necktie)

# Activity Thirty-Nine*

Warm-up

**Directions: Show the student the following three pictures.**

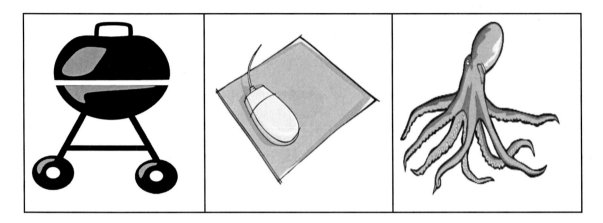

Ask: Look at the pictures. (grill, mousepad, octopus)
-Say *mousepad* backwards. (padmouse)
-Say *octopus* without the *pus*. (octo)
-Add *gon* to the end of *octo*. (octagon)
-How many syllables are in each of these words? (1, 2, 3)
-Give a word that rhymes with *grill*.

Use Elkonin boxes and have the student do the following:
    -Use chips to show the sounds in *grill*. (4)
    -Delete the /g/ in *grill*. (rill)
    -Change the /r/ in *rill* to /t/. (till)
    -Add /s/ to the beginning of *till*. (still)
    -Add *life* to the end of *still*. (still life)

Part II

**Syllable Substitution**
Say *boldness*. Instead of *bold* say *damp*. (dampness)
Say *remind*. Instead of *mind*, say *spect*. (respect)
Say *middle*. Instead of *mid*, say *fid*. (fiddle)
Say *curfew*. Instead of *cur* say *neph*. (nephew)
Say *keypad*. Instead of *pad* say *punch*. (keypunch)

**Middle Sound Identification**
What is the middle sound in *fight*? (/ī/)
What is the middle sound in *rip*? (/ĭ/)
What is the middle sound in *chalk*? (/aw/)

# Activity Forty*

Warm-up

**Directions: Show the student the following three pictures.**

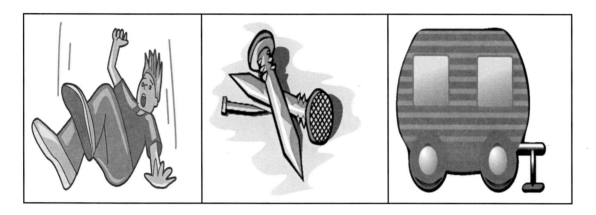

Ask: Look at the pictures. (slip, nail, trailer)
-Which two words have blends in them? What are they? (slip-/sl/, trailer-/tr/)
-Which two words have the same vowel sound? (nail, trailer-/ā/)
-How many syllables are in each of these words? (1, 1, 2)
-Give a word that rhymes with *nail*.

Use Elkonin boxes and have the student do the following:
    -Use chips to show the sounds in *slip*. (4)
    -Delete the /s/ in *slip*. (lip)
    -Change the /p/ to /t/. (lit)
    -Add *moon* to the beginning of *lit*. (moonlit)
    -Reverse the syllables in *moonlit*. (litmoon)
    -Take off the *lit* and put on *full*. (full moon)

Part II

**Rhyme Generation**
Give two words that rhyme with *strap*.
Give two words that rhyme with *fine*.
Give two words that rhyme with *school*.
Give two words that rhyme with *train*.
Give two words that rhyme with *vase*.

**Syllable Addition**
Add *pub* to the beginning of *lick*. (public)
Add *ton* to the beginning of *sil*. (tonsil)
Add *spot* to the end of *sun*. (sunspot)
Add *tile* to the end of *rep*. (reptile)

# Activity Forty-One*

Warm-up

**Directions: Show the student the following three pictures.**

Ask: Look at the pictures. (skate, yarn, vase)
-Which word has a blend in it? What is it? (skate-/sk/)
-Which two words have the same vowel sound? (vase, skate-/ā/)
-How many syllables are in each of these words? (1, 1, 1)
-Give a word that rhymes with *yarn*.

Use Elkonin boxes and have the student do the following:
    -Use chips to show the sounds in *skate*. (4)
    -Delete the /s/ in *skate*. (Kate)
    -Change the /ā/ in *Kate* to /ī/. (kite)
    -Change the /k/ in *kite* to /s/. (sight)
    -Add *eye* to the beginning of *sight*. (eyesight)

Part II

**Sound Substitution**
Say *resign*. Instead of /r/, say /d/. (design)
Say *least*. Instead of /l/, say /b/. (beast)
Say *rest*. Instead of /r/, say /b/. (best)
Say *damp*. Instead of /d/, say /l/. (lamp)
Say *light*. Instead of /l/, say /f/. (fight)

**Sound Deletion**
Say *jump* without the /j/. (ump)
Say *for* without the /f/. (or)
Say *shingle* without the /sh/. (ingle)
Say *bake* without /b/. (ache)

# Activity Forty-Two*

Warm-up

**Directions: Show the student the following three pictures.**

Ask: Look at the pictures. (scissors, unicorn, fries)
-Which word has a blend in it? What is it? (fries-/fr/)
-Which two words end with the same sound? (scissors, fries-/z/)
-How many syllables are in each of these words? (2, 3, 1)
-Say *unicorn* without corn. (uni)
-Give a word that rhymes with *fries*.

Use Elkonin boxes and have the student do the following:
    -Use chips to show the sounds in *corn*. (3)
    -Change the /n/ in *corn* to /k/. (cork)
    -Change the /or/ in *cork* to /i/. (kick)
    -Add *ball* to the end of *kick*. (kickball)
    -Reverse the syllables in *kickball*. (ballkick)

Part II

**Syllable Reversal**
Reverse the syllables in *sublet*. (letsub)
Reverse the syllables in *midyear*. (yearmid)
Reverse the syllables in *thumbtack*. (tackthumb)
Reverse the syllables in *orchid*. (kidor)
Reverse the syllables in *goblet*. (letgob)

**Syllable Substitution**
Say *pardon*. Instead of *don* say /tē/. (party)
Say *workout*. Instead of *out* say *place*. (workplace)
Say *earthquake*. Instead of *quake* say *worm*. (earthworm)

# Activity Forty-Three*

Warm-up

**Directions: Show the student the following three pictures.**

Ask: Look at the pictures. (parasail, tattoo, fright)
-Which word has a blend in it? (fright-/fr/)
-Which word has the least syllables? (fright)
-Which word has the most syllables? (parasail-3)
-Say *parachute* without the *sail*. (para)
-Give a word that rhymes with *fright*.

Use Elkonin boxes and have the student do the following:
    -Use chips to show the sounds in *fright*. (4)
    -Delete the /t/ in *fright*. (fry)
    -Add *french* to the beginning of *fry*. (french –fry)
    -Reverse the syllables in *french–fry*. (fryfrench)
    -Delete *fry* from *fry french*. (french)
    -Add *toast* to the end of *french*. (french toast)

## Part II

**Initial Consonant Identification**
Which word begins with the same first sound you hear in *pace*?
late        paper        stuck        (paper)
Which word begins with the same first sound you hear in *decide*?
drag        knife        jail        (drag)
Which word begins with the same first sound you hear in *fable*?
vein        table        famous        (famous)

**Rhyme Generation**
Give two words that rhyme with *bent.*

# Activity Forty-Four*

Warm-up

**Directions: Show the student the following three pictures.**

Ask: Look at the pictures. (slate, frame, hose)
-Which two words have blends in them? What are they? (slate-/sl/, frame-/fr/)
-Which two words have the same vowel sound? (frame, slate-/ā/)
-How many syllables are in each of these words? (1, 1, 1)
-Give a word that rhymes with *hose*.

Use Elkonin boxes and have the student do the following:
    -Use chips to show the sounds in *slate*. (4)
    -Delete the /s/ in *slate*. (late)
    -Add /p/ to the beginning of *late*. (plate)
    -Add *dinner* to the end of *plate*. (platedinner)
    -Reverse the words in *platedinner*. (dinnerplate)

## Psrt II

**Hidden Syllables**
Is the syllable *air* in the word *airplane*? (y)
pathway? (n)
airmail? (y)
spray? (n)
airway? (y)


**Final Sound Generation**
Think of a word that ends with the same last sound you hear in *cost*.
Think of a word that ends with the same last sound you hear in *stall*.
Think of a word that ends with the same last sound you hear in *pumpkin*.

# Activity Forty-Five*

Warm-up

**Directions: Show the student the following three pictures.**

Ask: Look at the pictures. (yolk, yak, stork)
-Which two words begin with the same sound? (yolk, yak-/y/)
-How many syllables are in each of these words? (1, 1, 1)
-Which word begins with a blend? (stork-/st/)
-Give a word that rhymes with *yak*.

Use Elkonin boxes and have the student do the following:
    -Use chips to show the sounds in *yak*. (3)
    -Change the /y/ in *yak* to /b/. (back)
    -Add *pack* to the end of *back*. (backpack)
    -Reverse the syllables in *backpack*. (packback)
    -Change *back* to *et*. (packet)

Part II

**Sound Segmentation**
Tap out the sounds in *flip*. (/f/ /l/ /i/ /p/)
Tap out the sounds in *baste*. (/b/ /ā/ /s/ /t/ )
Tap out the sounds in *first*. (/f/ /ir/ /s/ /t/)
Tap out the sounds in *needle*. (/n/ /ē/ /d/ /l/)
Tap out the sounds in *place*. (/p/ /l/ /ā/ /s/)

**Syllable Addition**
Add *did* to the end of *out*. (outdid)
Add *too* to the beginning of *ter*. (tutor)
Add /chur/ to the end of /crea/. (creature)
Add *it* to the end of /gran/. (granite)

# Activity Forty-Six*

Warm-up

**Directions: Show the student the following three pictures.**

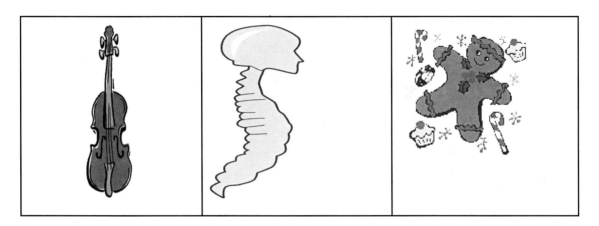

Ask: Look at the pictures. (violin, spine, gingerbread man)
-Which word begins with a blend? (spine-/sp/)
-Which two words have the same long vowel sound? (violin, spine-ī)
-How many syllables are in each of these words? (3, 1, 4)
-Give a word that rhymes with *spine*.

Use Elkonin boxes and have the student do the following:
    -Use chips to show the sounds in *spine*. (4)
    -Delete the /s/ in *spine*. (pine)
    -Change the /n/ in *pine* to /l/. (pile)
    -Add *pig* to the beginning of *pile*. (pigpile)
    -Reverse the syllables in *pig pile*. (pilepig)

Part II

**Sound Match**
Does *trap* end with /p/ or /b/? (/p/)
Does *cupid* end with /d/ or /b/? (/d/)
Does *harsh* end with /sh/ or /ch/? (/sh/)
Does *baby* end with /ee/ or /ī/? (/ee/)
Does *water* end with /e/ or /r/? (/r/)

**Rhyme Identification**
| | | | | |
|---|---|---|---|---|
| Which word rhymes with *grape*? | gain | stop | tape | (tape) |
| Which word rhymes with *vase*? | pace | take | lap | (pace) |
| Which word rhymes with *guest*? | rent | pest | beat | (pest) |
| Which word rhymes with *mild*? | chill | mint | child | (child) |

# Activity Forty-Seven*

Warm-up

**Directions: Show the student the following three pictures.**

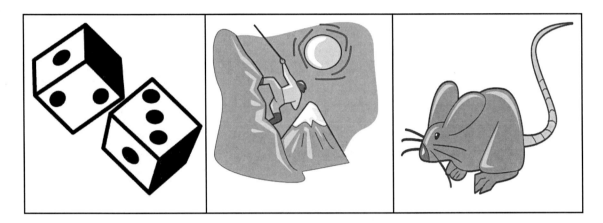

Ask: Look at the pictures. (dice, climb, mouse)
-Which word has a blend in it? (climb-/cl/)
-Which two words have the same vowel sound? (dice, climb-/ī/)
-Which two words end with the same sound? (dice, mouse-/s/)
-How many syllables are in each of these words? (1, 1, 1)
-Give a word that rhymes with *dice*.

Use Elkonin boxes and have the student do the following:
    -Use chips to show the sounds in *mouse*. (3)
    -Change the /s/ in *mouse* to /th/. (mouth)
    -Add *loud* to the beginning of *mouth*. (loudmouth)
    -Reverse the syllables in *loudmouth*. (mouth loud)

Part II

**Rhyme Generation**
Give two words that rhyme with *time*.
Give two words that rhyme with *shrimp*.
Give two words that rhyme with *plow*.
Give two words that rhyme with *gleam*.
Give two words that rhyme with *groan*.

**Sound Isolation**
What sound do you hear in *past* that's missing in *pass*? (/t/)
What sound do you hear in *rushed* that's missing in *rush*? (/t/)
What sound do you hear in *train* that's missing in *tray*? (/n/)
What sound do you hear in *place* that's missing in *play*? (/s/)

# Activity Forty-Eight*

Warm-up

**Directions: Show the student the following three pictures.**

Ask: Look at the pictures. (dart, sled, telephone)
-Which word has a blend in it? (sled-/sl/)
-Which two words have the same vowel sound? (sled, telephone-/ĕ/)
-How many syllables are in each of these words? (1, 1, 3)
-Give a word that rhymes with *sled*.

Use Elkonin boxes and have the student do the following:
    -Use chips to show the sounds in *dart*. (3)
    -Change the /d/ in *dart* to /t/. (tart)
    -Add /s/ to the beginning of *tart*. (start)
    -Change the final /t/ in *start* to /k/. (stark)
    -Change the /ar/ in *stark* to /i/. (stick)

Part II

**Phoneme Substitution**
Say *waist*. Instead of /w/, say /p/. (paste)
Say *sand*. Instead of /s/, say /b/. (band)
Say *slate*. Instead of /s/, say /p/. (plate)
Say *wind*. Instead of /w/, say /b/. (bind)
Say *choose*. Instead of /ch/, say /l/. (lose)

**Rhyme Identification**
Which word rhymes with *came*?    stay      blame      tramp      (blame)
Which word rhymes with *taste*?    haste      train      tack      (haste)
Which word rhymes with *boast*?    coast      coat      cone      (coast)

# Activity Forty-Nine*

Warm-up

**Directions: Show the student the following three pictures.**

Ask: Look at the pictures. (inch, igloo, peach)
-Which two words end with the same sound? (inch, peach-/ch/)
-Which two words have the same vowel sound? (inch, igloo-/i/)
-How many syllables are in each of these words? (1, 2, 1)
-Give a word that rhymes with *peach*.

Use Elkonin boxes and have the student do the following:
    -Use chips to show the sounds in *peach*. (3)
    -Change the /ch/ in *peach* to /s/. (peace)
    -Change the /p/ in *peace* to /l/. (lease)
    -Change the /s/ in *lease* to /p/. (leap)
    -Add *frog* to the end of *leap*. (leapfrog)

Part II

**Sound Recognition**
Does *wilt* have three sounds? (no-4)
Does *smoke* have four sounds? (y)
Does *scrape* have four sounds? (n-5)
Does *jump* have three sounds? (n-4)
Does *blame* have four sounds? (y)

**Sound Isolation**
What sound do you hear in *rake* that's missing in *ache*? (/r/)
What sound do you hear in *lame* that's missing in *aim*? (/l/)
What sound do you hear in *cinch* that's missing in *inch*? (/s/)
What sound do you hear in *pout* that's missing in *out*? (/p/)
What sound do you hear in *Pete* that's missing in *eat*? (/p/)

# Activity Fifty*

Warm-up

**Directions: Show the student the following three pictures.**

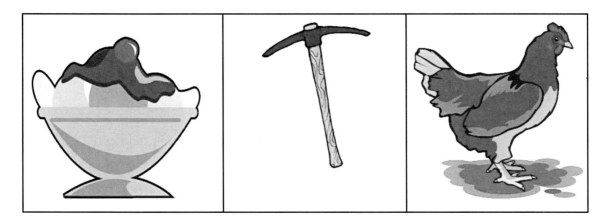

Ask: Look at the pictures. (ice cream, pick, chicken)
-Which word has a digraph at the beginning of it? (chicken-/ch/)
-Which two words have the same vowel sound? (pick, chicken-/i/)
-How many syllables are in each of these words? (2, 1, 2)
-Give a word that rhymes with *cream.*

Use Elkonin boxes and have the student do the following:
    -Use chips to show the sounds in *pick.* (3)
    -Change the /k/ in *pick* to /l/. (pill)
    -Add /s/ to the beginning of *pill.* (spill)
    -Add /d/ to the end of *spill.* (spilled)
    -Add *milk* to the end of *spilled.* (spilled milk)

Part II

**Sentence Segmentation**
Count the words in the following sentences:
The dog wagged his tail. (5)
The beautiful flowers are wilting. (5)
The cat meowed and purred. (5)
The city trucks are loaded with sand. (7)

**Segmenting Initial Sounds in Words**
What's the first sound you hear in *safety.* (/s/)
What's the first sound you hear in *smart*? (/s/)
What's the first sound you hear in *night*? (/n/)
What's the first sound you hear in *even*? (/ē/)

# Level Two Activities

# Activity One***

Warm-up

**Directions: Show the student the following three pictures.**

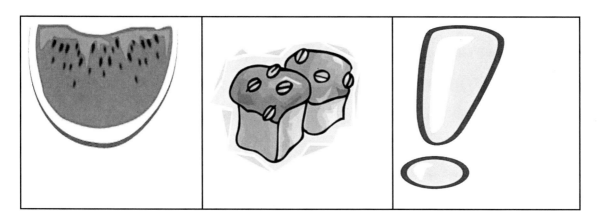

Ask: Look at the pictures. (watermelon, muffin, exclamation)
-What sound do all the pictures end with? (/n/)
-How many syllables are in each of these words? (4, 2, 4)
-Say *watermelon* without the *on*. (watermel)
-Delete the second syllable in *watermel*. (wamel)
-Say *melwater*. Instead of *water* say *vin*. (Melvin)

Use Elkonin boxes if necessary, and have the student do the following:
Show the syllables in *exclamation*. (4)
Delete the first syllable. (clumation)
Delete the second syllable in *clumation*. (clution)
Reverse the syllables in *clution*. (tionclu)
Delete the first syllable in *tionclu*. (clu)

Part II

**Syllable Deletion**
Say *cliffhanger* without *cliff*. What's left? (hanger)
Say *chipmunk* without *munk*. What's left? (chip)
Say *dramatize* without *tize*. What's left? (drama)
Say *earthling* without *ling*. What's left? (earth)
Say *alligator* without *al*. What's left? (igator)

**Sound Deletion**
Say *pursuit* without the /t/.     (pursue)
Say *blue* without the /l/.     (boo)
Say *gasp* without the /p/.     (gas)

# Activity Two***

Warm-up

**Directions: Show the student the following three pictures.**

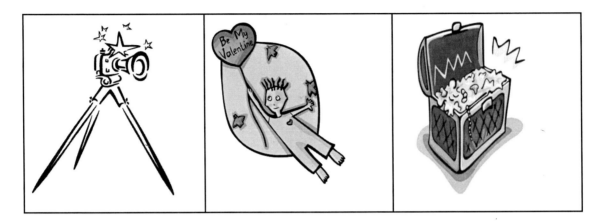

Ask: Look at the pictures. (flash, float, chest)
-Which two words end with the same sound? (float, chest)
-What digraphs do you hear in *flash* and *chest*? (/sh/, /ch/)
-What blends are in these words? (/fl/, /fl/, /st/)
-Give another word that rhymes with *float*.

Use Elkonin boxes and have the student do the following:
    -Use the chips to show the sounds in the word *chest*. (4)
    -Delete the last sound in *chest*. What's left? (chess)
    -Change the /ch/ in *chess* to /l/. What's the new word? (less)
    -Add *fruit* to the beginning of *less*. (fruitless)

Part II

**Sound Isolation**
What sound do you hear in *window* that's not in *wind*? (/ō/)
What sound do you hear in *time* that's not in *tie*? (/m/)
What sound do you hear in *brown* that's not in *brow*? (/n/)
What sound do you hear in *paint* that's not in *pain*? (/t/)
What sound do you hear in *style* that's not in *sty*? (/l/)

**Syllable Substitution**
Say *voicemail*. Instead of *mail*, say *box*. (voicebox)
Say *landscape*. Instead of *scape* say *fill*. (landfill)
Say *scapegoat*. Instead of *scape* say *billy*. (billygoat)
Say *flashlight*. Instead of *flash* say *spot*. (spotlight)
Say *motel*. Instead of *tel* say *ment*. (moment)

# Activity Three***

Warm-up

**Directions: Show the student the following three pictures.**

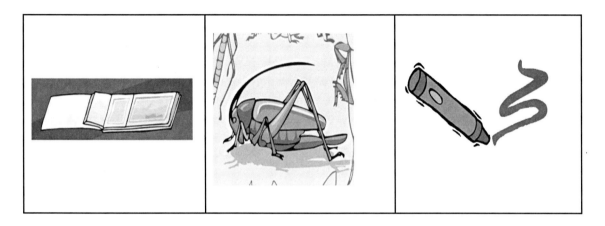

Ask: Look at the pictures. (checkbook, grasshopper, crayon)
-How many syllables are in each word? (2, 3, 2)
-What digraph do you hear at the beginning of checkbook? (/ch/)
-Where are the blends in the words *crayon* and *grasshopper*? (beginning)
-Say *crayon* without *on*. (cray)
-Add *fish* to the end of *cray*. (crayfish)

Use Elkonin boxes and have the student do the following:
    -Use the chips to show the syllables in *grasshopper*. (3)
    -Take off the first syllable in *grasshopper*. What's left? (hopper)
    -Take off the second syllable in *grasshopper*. What's left? (grasser)

Part II

**Rhyme Identification**
Ask: "Do these words rhyme?"
| | | |
|---|---|---|
| flame | plane | (n) |
| crank | bank | (y) |
| mountain | jumping | (n) |
| stale | shale | (y) |
| cover | clover | (n) |

**Syllable Reversal** (Use Elkonin boxes if necessary.)
Reverse the syllables in *drainpipe*. (pipedrain)
Reverse the syllables in *baboon*. (boonba)
Reverse the syllables in *protein*. (teinpro)
Reverse the syllables in *biscuit*. (kitbis)

# Activity Four***

Warm-up

**Directions: Show the student the following three pictures.**

Ask: Look at the pictures. (crash, goldfish, grapes)
-Which word has the most syllables in it? How many? (goldfish-2)
-What two words end with the same sound? (goldfish, crash)
-Give a word that rhymes with *grape*.
-Where is the blend in the word *crash*? (beginning-/cr/)

Use Elkonin boxes and have the student do the following:
- Use the chips to show the sounds in crash. (4)
- Delete the first sound. What's left? (rash)
- Delete the second sound in *crash*. What's left? (cash)
- Now change the /k/ in *cash* to /d/. What's your new word? (dash)
- Add *mad* to the beginning of *dash*. (mad dash)

Part II

**Sound Deletion**
Say *feast* without the /s/. (feet)
Say *curdle* without the /d/. (curl)
Say *earthly* without the /l/. (earthy)
Say *cluster* without the /s/. (clutter)
Say *splint* without the /n/. (split)

**Final Sound Substitution**
Say *bust*. Instead of /t/ say /l/. (bustle)
Say *class*. Instead of /s/, say /p/. (clap)
Say *cloak*. Instead of the last /k/ say /n/. (clone)
Say *slim*. Instead of /m/, say /p/. (slip)

# Activity Five***

Warm-up

Directions: Show the student the following pictures.

Ask: Look at the pictures. (motorcycle, merry-go-round, mule)
-Which two words have the same number of syllables? How many? (motorcycle, merry
  -go-round-4)
-What sound do all three words have in common? (/m/)
-What ending sound is the same in two words? (/l/)

Use Elkonin boxes and have the student do the following:
    -Use the chips to show the sounds in *mule*. (3)
    -Change the first sound in *mule* to /r/. (rule)
    -Add /d/ to the beginning of *rule*. (drool)
    -How many sounds in *drool*? (4)
Part II

**Sound Isolation**
What sound do you hear in *power* that's missing in *our*? (/p/)
What sound do you hear in *ground* that's missing in *round*? (/g/)
What sound do you hear in *tame* that's missing in *aim*? (/t/)
What sound do you hear in *box* that's missing in *ox*? (/b/)
What sound do you hear in *blink* that's missing in *link*? (/b/)
What sound do you hear in *branch* that's missing in *ranch*? (/b/)

**Word Switch**
Reverse the words.
*danger zone* (zone danger)
*runway* (way run)
*pin cushion* (cushion pin)
*water cooler* (cooler water)
*home sick* (sick home)

# Activity Six***
Warm-up

**Directions: Show the student the following three pictures.**

Ask: Look at the pictures. (clarinet, steep, sweep)
-Which two words rhyme? (sweep, steep)
-How many syllables are in *clarinet*? (3)
-What are the blends at the beginning of each word? (/cl/, /st/, /sw/)
-What vowel do you hear in *steep* and *sweep*? (/ē/)

Use Elkonin boxes and have the student do the following:
    -Use the chips to show the sounds in *sweep*. (4)
    -Delete the first sound in *sweep*. (weep)
    -Change the /p/ in *weep* to /t/ (wheat)
    -Change the /ee/ in *wheat* to /ī/. (white)
    -Add *out* to the end of *white*. (whiteout)

Part II

## Sound Deletion
Say *thread* without the /th/. (red)
Say *sweater* without the /s/. (wetter)
Say *steady* without the /s/. (teddy)
Say *soil* without the /s/. (oil)
Say *dugout* without the /d/. (ugout)

## Syllable Substitution
Say_____. Instead of _____ say_____.

| | | | |
|---|---|---|---|
| landmark | mark | fill | landfill |
| dishpan | pan | towel | dishtowel |
| pocket | pock | mark | market |
| playground | ground | house | playhouse |
| tingle | tin | jun | jungle |

# Activity Seven***
Warm-up

**Directions: Show the student the following three pictures.**

Ask: Look at the pictures. (polarbear, pin, pig)
-Which word has the most syllables? (polarbear-3)
-Is the vowel sound the same in *pig* and *pin*? (yes) What is it? ( /i/)
-Give two words that rhyme with *pin*.
-Say *pin* backwards. (nip)

Use Elkonin boxes and have the student do the following:
    -Use the chips to show the syllables in *polarbear*. (3)
    -Delete the second syllable in *polar bear*. What's left? (pobear)
    -Move the first syllable in *polar bear* to the end. What's the new word? (larbearpo)
    -Take *bearpo* off *larbearpo* and add /j/. (large)

Part II

## Sound Isolation
What sound do you hear in *bellow* that's not in *bell*? (ō)
What sound do you hear in *surf* that's not in *sir*? (/f/)
What sound do you hear in *scorch* that's not in *score*? (/ch/)
What sound do you hear in *storm* that's not in *store*? (/m/)
What sound do you hear in *lamp* that's not in *lamb*? (/p/)

## Phoneme Substitution
Say _____. Take off the ____; put in a _____.
    flashed            /f/            /s/          (slashed)
    clamped          /l/           /r/          (cramped)
    round              /ou/         /ā/          (rained)

# Activity Eight***

Warm-up

**Directions: Show the student the following three pictures.**

Ask: Look at the pictures. (flipper, flower, clown)
-Which two words have the same beginning sound? (flipper, flower-/f/)
-What blends do you hear at the beginning of each of these words? (/fl/, /cl/)
-Give a word that rhymes with *flower*.

Use Elkonin boxes and have the student do the following:
    -Use chips to show the sounds in *clown*. (4)
    -Change the /l/ in *clown* to /r/. (crown)
    -Change the /k/ in *crown* to /b/. (brown)
    -Delete the /n/ in *brown*. (brow)
    -Add *eye* to the beginning of *brow*. (eyebrow)

Part II

**Initial Sound Deletion**
Say *poodle* without the /p/. (oodle)
Say *school* without the /s/. (cool)
Say *sport* without the /s/. (port)
Say *troll* without the /t/. (roll)
Say *scope* without the /s/. (cope)

**Final Sound Deletion**
Say *drawl* without the /l/. (draw)
Say *grate* without the /t/. (gray)
Say *scorn* without the /n/. (score)
Say *noisy* without the /ē/. (noise)
Say *chuckle* without /l/. (chuck)

# Activity Nine***

Warm-up

**Directions: Show the student the following three pictures.**

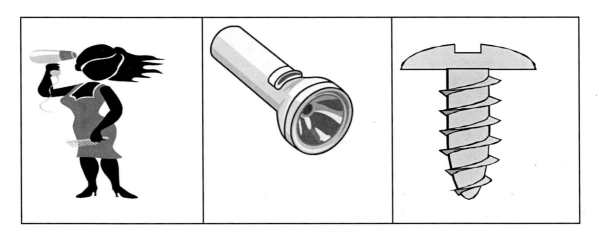

Ask: Look at the pictures. (blew, flashlight, screw)
-What two words have the same ending sound? (blew, screw-/oo/)
-What blends do you hear at the beginning of each of these words? (/bl/, /fl/, /scr/)
-How many syllables are in each word? (1, 2, 1)
-Give a word that rhymes with *blew*.

Use Elkonin boxes and have the student do the following:
    -Use chips to show the sounds in *blew*. (3)
    -Delete the /b/ in *blew*. (loo)
    -Add /s/ to the end of *loo*. (loose)
    -Add *foot* to the beginning of loose. (footloose)
    -Reverse the syllables in *footloose*. (loose foot)
    -Change the *foot* in *loosefoot* to *lips*. (loose lips)

Part II

**Segmentation of Vowel Sounds**
What's the vowel sound in *please*? (/ē/)
What's the vowel sound in *chunk*? (/ŭ/)
What's the vowel sound in *trail*. (/ā/)
What's the vowel sound in *trench*? (/ĕ/)
What's the vowel sound in *stooge*? (/oo/)

**Initial Sound Isolation**
What's the first sound you hear in *strip*? (/s/)
What's the first sound you hear in *grapple*? (/g/)

# Activity Ten ***

Warm-up

**Directions: Show the student the following three pictures.**

Ask: Look at the pictures. (extinguisher, elephant, scratch)
-How many syllables are in each word? (4, 3, 1)
-What blend do you hear at the beginning of *scratch*? (/scr/)
-Say *extinguisher* without the last syllable. (extinguish)
-Give a word that rhymes with *scratch*.

Use Elkonin boxes and have the student do the following:
    -Use chips to show the sounds in *scratch*. (5)
    -Delete the /s/ in *scratch*. (cratch)
    -Change the /ă/ in *cratch* to /ŭ/. (crutch)
    -Add /iz/ to the end of *crutch*. (crutches)

Part II

**Syllable Reversal**
Add *hole* to the end of *knot*. (knothole)
Add *for* to the end of *sake*. (sakefor)
Add *go* to the end of *car*. (cargo)
Add *hun* to the end of *gry*. (gryhun)
Add *chit* to the end of *chat*. (chatchit)

**Matching Final Sound to Word**
Does *stink* end with /n/ or /k/? (/k/)
Does *wrench* end with /th/ or /ch/? (/ch/)
Does *pretty* end with /ē/ or /ī/? (/ē/)
Does *plastic* end with /k/ or /t/? (/k/)

# Activity Eleven***

Warm-up

**Directions: Show the student the following three pictures.**

Ask: Look at the pictures. (handcuff, armadillo, hoe)
-How many syllables are in each of these words? (2, 4, 1)
-Say *handcuff* without *hand*. (cuff)
-Add /s/ to the beginning of *cuff*. (scuff)
-Change the /ŭ/ in *scuff* to /ĭ/. (skiff)

Use Elkonin boxes if necessary and have the student do the following:
    -Use chips to show the sounds in *hoe*. (2)
    -Add /p/ to the end of *hoe*. (hope)
    -Add *full* to the end of *hope*. (hopeful)
    -Reverse the syllables in *hopeful*. (fullhope)
    -Change *hope* in *full hope* to *body*. (fullbody)

Part II

**Rhyme Generation**
Give two words that rhyme with *yellow*.
Give two words that rhyme with *crowd*.
Give two words that rhyme with *bumble*.
Give two words that rhyme with *faint*.

**Sound Deletion**
Say *plain* without the /l/. (pain)
Say *scoop* without the /k/. (soup)
Say *stickle* without the /t/. (sickle)
Say *blurt* without the /l/. (Bert)

# Activity Twelve***

Warm-up

**Directions: Show the student the following three pictures.**

Ask: Look at the pictures. (scooter, scarf, skeleton)
-What blend is the same in each of these words? (/sk/)
-How many syllables are in the word s*keleton*? (3)
-Say *scooter* without the *er*. (scoot)
-Give a word that rhymes with *scoot*.

Use Elkonin boxes and have the student do the following:
    -Use chips to show the sounds in *scarf*. (4)
    -Delete the /f/ in *scarf*. (scar)
    -Add /p/ to the end of *scar*. (scarp)
    -Change the /ar/ in scarp to /i/. (skip)
    -Add *rope* to the end of *skip*. (skip rope)

Part II

**Syllable Deletion**
Say *chandelier* without *del*. (chanier)
Say *hydroplane* without *dro*. (hyplane)
Say *expensive* without *pen*. (exsive)
Say *fugitive* without *git*. (fu-ive)
Say *impulsive* without *pul*. (imsive)

**Supply Initial Sound in Words**
What sound do you hear in *secretive* that's missing in ecretive? (/s/)
What sound do you hear in *grateful* that's missing in rateful? (/g/)
What sound do you hear in *snob* that's missing in *knob*? (/s/)
What sound do you hear in *swimmer* that's missing in *wimmer*? (/s/)

# Activity Thirteen***

Warm-up

**Directions: Show the student the following three pictures.**

Ask: Look at the pictures. (platypus, street, kilt)
-What two words have the same ending sound? (street, kilt)
-What blends do you hear at the beginning of two of these words? (/pl/, /str/)
-How many syllables are in *platypus*? (3)
-Say *platypus* without /ə/. (platpus)
-Say *platpus*. Instead of *pus* say *form*. (platform)

Use Elkonin boxes and have the student do the following:
    -Use chips to show the sounds in *kilt*. (4)
    -Take off the /t/. (kill)
    -Add a /s/ to the beginning of *kill*. (skill)
    -Add a /d/ to the end of *skill*. (skilled)

Part II

**Substituting Vowel Sounds in Words**
Say *batter*. Instead of /ă/, say /ĭ/. (bitter)
Say *blurb*. Instead of /ur/, say /ŏ/. (blob)
Say *shark*. Instead of /ar/, say /oo/. (shook)
Say *crimp*. Instead of /ĭ/, say /ă/. (cramp)
Say *flush*. Instead of /ŭ/ say /ă/. (flash)

**Segmenting Final Sounds in Words**
What's the last sound you hear in *scratch*? (/ch/)
What's the last sound you hear in *envelope*? (/p/)
What's the last sound you hear in *scorched*? (/t/)
What's the last sound you hear in *submission*? (/n/)
What's the last sound you hear in *terrible*? (/l/)

# Activity Fourteen***

Warm-up

**Directions: Show the student the following three pictures.**

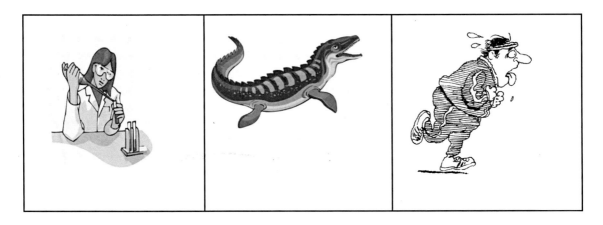

Ask: Look at the pictures. (experiment, alligator, sweat)
-Which two words have the same ending sound? (experiment, sweat-/t/)
-What blend do you hear at the beginning of *sweat*? (/sw/)
-What sounds do *experiment* and *alligator* begin with? (/e/, /a/)
-Give a word that rhymes with *sweat*.
-How many syllables are in each of these words? (4, 4, 1)

Use Elkonin boxes if needed and have the student do the following:
    -Use chips to show the sounds in *sweat*. (4)
    -Change the /e/ in *sweat* to /ē/. (sweet)
    -Delete the /s/ in *sweet*. (wheat)
    -Change the /t/ in *wheat* to /l/. (wheel)
    -Change the /w/ in *wheel* to /p/. (peel)
    -Say *peel* backwards. (leap)

Part II

**Substituting Initial Sounds in Words**
Say *pollute*. Instead of /p/, say /b/. (bollute)
Say *costume*. Instead of /k/, say /z/. (zostume)
Say *likewise*. Instead of /l/, say /m/. (mikewise)
Say *grapevine*. Instead of /g/, say /p/. (prapevine)

**Syllable Reversal**
Say *lifeboat* backwards. (boatlife)
Say *pretzel* backwards. (zelpret)

# Activity Fifteen***

Warm-up

**Directions: Show the student the following three pictures.**

Ask: Look at the pictures. (shark, hyena, shiver)
-Which two words have the same beginning sound? (shark, shiver-/sh/)
-How many syllables are in *hyena*? (3)
-Say *hyena* without the /ŭ/. (hyēn)
-Find a word that rhymes with *shark*.

Use Elkonin boxes and have the student do the following:
    -Use chips to show the syllables in *shiver*. (2)
    -Add /ing/ to the end of *shiver*. (shivering)
    -Change /shiv/ to /cov/ . (covering)
    -Change /ing/ to /d/. (covered)

Part II

**Segmenting Middle Sound in Words**
What's the middle sound in *pain*? (/ā/)?
What's the middle sound in *top*? (/ŏ/)
What's the middle sound in *goop*? (/oo/)
What's the middle sound in *jean*? (/ē/)
What's the middle sound in *fig*? (/ĭ/)

**Sound Switcheroo**
Reverse the first sounds in the following words.
*pillow top*          (tillow pop)
*jump rope*          (rump jope)
*teacher's pet*       (peachers tet)

# Activity Sixteen***

Warm-up

**Directions: Show the student the following three pictures.**

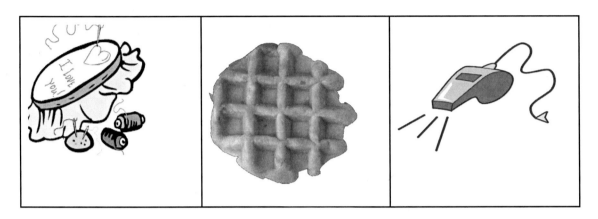

Ask: Look at the pictures. (embroidery, waffle, whistle)
-Which two words have the same ending sound? (waffle, whistle-/l/)
-What is the first vowel sound you hear in each of these words? (/e/, /o/, /i/)
-How many syllables are in each of these words? (4, 2, 2)
-Say *embroidery* without the third syllable. (embroidy)

Use Elkonin boxes and have the student do the following:
    -Use chips to show the sounds in *waffle*. (4)
    -Change the /f/ in *waffle* to /t/. (wattle)
    -Delete the /l/ from *wattle*. (watt)
    -Add /s/ to the beginning of *watt*. (swat)

Part II

**Supplying Final Sounds in Words**
What sound do you hear in *frame* that's missing in *fray*? (/m/)
What sound do you hear in *bunker* that's missing in *bunk*? (/er/)
What sound do you hear in *gold* that's missing in *goal*? (/d/)
What sound do you hear in *guest* that's missing in *guess*? (/t/)
What sound do you hear in *work* that's missing in *were*? (/k/)

**Substituting Initial Sounds**
Say *thresh*. Instead of /th/ say /f/. (fresh)
Say *flab*. Instead of /f/, say /b/. (blab)
Say *flame*. Instead of /f/, say /b/. (blame)
Say *bride*. Instead of /b/, say /p/. (pride)
Say *crime*. Instead of /k/, say /g/. (grime)

# Activity Seventeen***

Warm-up

**Directions: Show the student the following three pictures.**

Ask: Look at the pictures. (popcorn, spaghetti, splash)
-What word has the most syllables in it? (spaghetti-3)
-What blends do you hear at the beginning of *spaghetti* and *splash*? (/sp/, /spl/)
-Say *popcorn* backwards. (cornpop)
-Change the *pop* in *cornpop* to *cob*. (corncob)
-Give a word that rhymes with *splash*.

Use Elkonin boxes and have the student do the following:
    -Use chips to show the sounds in *splash*. (5)
    -Change the /sh/ in *splash* to /t/. (splat)
    -Change the /ă/ in *splat* to /ĭ/. (split).
    -Add *banana* to the beginning of *split*. (banana split)
    -Reverse the words of *banana split*. (split banana)

Part II

**Segmenting Sounds in Words**
Tap out the sounds you hear in *strap*. (/s/ /t/ /r/ /a/ /p/)
Tap out the sounds you hear in *thrive*. (/th/ /r/ /ī/ /v/)
Tap out the sounds you hear in *blunt*. (/b/ /l/ /u/ /n/ /t/)
Tap out the sounds you hear in *stream*. (/s/ /t/ /r/ /ē/ /m/)
Tap out the sounds you hear in *gossip*. (/g/ /o/ /s/ /i/ /p/)

**Sound Discrimination**
Are the vowel sounds in *staff* and *black* the same? (y) What is the vowel sound? (/ă/)
Are the vowel sounds in *join* and *cow* the same? (n)
Are the vowel sounds in *grin* and *step* the same? (n)

# Activity Eighteen***

Warm-up

**Directions: Show the student the following three pictures.**

Ask: Look at the pictures. (kayak, koala, snail)
-What two words have the same beginning sound? (kayak, koala)
-How many syllables are there in *koala*? (3)
-What blend do you hear at the beginning of *snail*? (/sn/)
-Find a word that rhymes with *snail*.

Use Elkonin boxes and have the student do the following:
    -Use chips to show the sounds in *snail*. (4)
    -Delete the /s/ in *snail*. (nail)
    -Change the /ā/ in *nail* to /ī/. (Nile)
    -Change the /n/ in *Nile* to /m/. (mile)
    -Add /s/ to the beginning of *mile*. (smile)

Part II

**Syllable Deleting**
Say *sunflower* without *flou*. (sunner)
Say *fantastic* without *tas*. (fantic)
Say *reliant* without *re*. (liant)
Say *genuine* without /ū/. (genin)
Say *catalogue* without the /ŭ/. (catlog)

**Sound Switcheroo**
Reverse the first sounds in *searchlight*. (learch sight)
Reverse the first sounds in *mountain*. (tounmen)
Reverse the first sounds in *forgot*. (gorfot)

# Activity Nineteen***

Warm-up

**Directions: Show the student the following three pictures.**

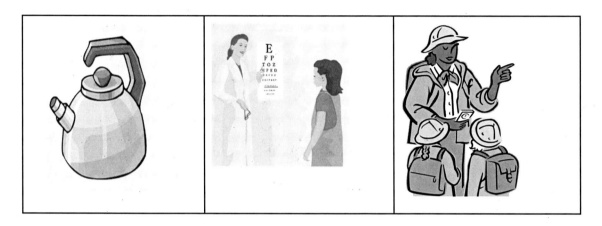

Ask: Look at the pictures. (kettle, optometrist, scout)
-Which two words have the same ending sound? (scout, optometrist-/t/)
-What blend do you hear at the beginning of *scout*? (/sk/)
-How many syllables are in each word? (2, 4, 1)
-Give a word that rhymes with *scout*.

Use Elkonin boxes and have the student do the following:
    -Use chips to show the sounds in *scout*. (4)
    -Change the /ou/ in *scout* to /i/. (skit)
    -Delete the /k/ in *skit*. (sit)
    -Add *baby* to the beginning of *sit*. (babysit)
    -Reverse the syllables in *babysit*. (sitbaby)

Part II

**Working With Beginning Blends**
Think of a word that begins with the blend (/sl/).
Think of a word that begins with the blend (/br/).
Think of a word that begins with the blend (/sn/).
Think of a word that begins with the blend (/cl/).
Think of a word that begins with the blend (/tr/).

**Substituting Final Sounds in Words**
Say *slim*. Instead of /m/ say /t/. (slit)
Say *branch*. Instead of /ch/, say /d/. (brand)
Say *screen*. Instead of /n/, say /ch/. (screech)
Say *pride*. Instead of /d/, say /m/. (prime)

# Activity Twenty***

Warm-up

**Directions: Show the student the following three pictures.**

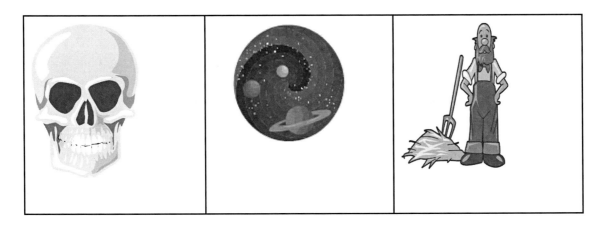

Ask: Look at the pictures. (skeleton, universe, straw)
-How many syllables are in each of these words? (3, 3, 1)
-What blend do you hear at the beginning of *skeleton* and *straw*? (/sk/, /str/)
-Say *universe* without *verse*. (uni)
-Add *form* to the end of uni. (uniform)
-Give a word that rhymes with *straw*.

Use Elkonin boxes and have the student do the following:
-Use chips to show the sounds in *straw*. (4)
-Delete the /r/ in *straw*. (staw)
-Add /b/ to the end of *staw*. (stawb)
-Change the /aw/ in *stawb* to /ă/. (stab)
-Say *stab* backwards. (bats)

Part II

**Segmenting Syllables**
How many syllables are in *hippopotamus*? (5)
How many syllables are in *concentration*? (4)
How many syllables are in *plant*? (1)
How many syllables are in *snowstorm*? (2)
How many syllables are in *ravioli*? (4)

**Syllable Substitution**
Say *gorgeous*. Instead of *jus*, say *illa*. (gorilla)
Say *nutball*. Instead of *ball* say *shell*. (nutshell)
Say *handsome*. Instead of *some* say *held*. (handheld)

# Activity Twenty-One***

Warm-up

**Directions: Show the student the following three pictures.**

Ask: Look at the pictures. (surfboarder, walrus, rattlesnake)
-How many syllables are in each of these words? (3, 2, 3)
-What vowel sounds do you hear in the first syllables of each of the words? (/ur/,/ŏ/ /ă/)
-Say *rattlesnake* backwards. (snake rattle)
-Say *snake rattle* without *snake*. (rattle)
-Give a word that rhymes with *rattle.*

Use Elkonin boxes and have the student do the following:
    -Use chips to show the sounds in *snake.* (4)
    -Change the /k/ in *snake* to /l/. (snail)
    -Change the /n/ in *snail* to /t/. (stale)
    -Change the /l/ in *stale* to /n/. (stain)
    -Change the /ā/ in *stain* to /ĭ/. (stin)
    -Say *stin* backwards. (nits)

Part II

**Syllable Substitution**
Say *cypress.* Instead of *press,* say *cle.* (cycle)
Say *document.* Instead of *doc,* say *pave.* (pave-u-ment)
Say *horsefly.* Instead of *horse*, say *fruit.* (fruitfly)
Say *grapefruit.* Instead of *fruit,* say *juice.* (grape juice)

**Phoneme Substitution**
Say *clouds.* Instead of /d/, say /n/. (clowns)
Say *stable.* Instead of /b/, say /p/. (staple)
Say *spider.* Instead of /p/, say /l/. (slider)

# Activity Twenty-Two***

Warm-up

**Directions: Show the student the following three pictures.**

Ask: Look at the pictures. (scrabble, sunshine, hippopotomus)
-What two words have the same number of syllables? (scrabble, sunshine-2)
-Which word has the most syllables? (hippopotomus-5)
-Which word has a blend, and what is it? (scrabble–/scr/)
-Say *sunshine* without *sun*. (shine)
-Give a word that rhymes with *shine.*

Use Elkonin boxes and have the student do the following:
    -Use chips to show the sounds in *shine*. (3)
    -Add /r/ after the /sh/ in *shine*. (shrine)
    -Change the /n/ in *shrine* to /m/. (shrime)
    -Change the /ī/ in shrime to /ĭ/. (shrim)
    -Add /p/ to the end of *shrim*. (shrimp)

Part II

**Syllable Reversal**
Switch the syllables in *neutral*. (tralneu)
Switch the syllables in *fabric*. (ricfab)
Switch the syllables in *exile*. (ile-ex)
Switch the syllables in *transfer*. (fertrans)
Switch the syllables in *display*. (playdis)

**Phoneme Deletion**
Say *stacked* without the first /t/. (sacked)
Say *scandal* without the /k/. (sandal)
Say *snack* without the /n/. (sack)

# Activity Twenty-Three***

Warm-up

**Directions: Show the student the following three pictures.**

Ask: Look at the pictures. (neighbor, toaster, newborn)
-Which two words have the same last sound? (neighbor, toaster)
-How many syllables are in each of the words? (2)
-Say *newborn* backwards. (born new)
-Reverse the first sound in each syllable of *new born*. (bew norn)
-Give a word that rhymes with *toast*.

Use Elkonin boxes and have the student do the following:
    -Use chips to show the sounds in *toast*. (4)
    -Delete the /s/ in *toast*. (tote)
    -Change the /ō/ in tote to /ī/. (tight)
    -Add *end* to the end of *tight*. (tight end)
    -Change *tight* in *tight end* to /s/. (send)

Part II

**Syllable Substitution**
Say *consistent*. Instead of *con*, say *per*. (persistent)
Say *drybrush*. Instead of *brush,* say *rot*. (dryrot)
Say *contain*. Instead of *tain*, say *tent*. (content)
Say *inside*. Instead of *side,* say *stinct*. (instinct)
Say *image*. Instead of *ij,* say *part*. (impart)

**Sound Substitution**
Say *purchase*. Instead of /ch/, say /p/. (purpose)
Say *tulip*. Instead of /l/, say /n/. (tunip)
Say *coast*. Instead of /s/, say /l/. (colt)
Say *collect*. Instead of /l/, say /n/. (connect)

# Activity Twenty-Four***

Warm-up

**Directions: Show the student the following three pictures.**

Ask: Look at the pictures. (iguana, necktie, octagon)
-How many syllables are in each of the words? (3, 2, 3)
-Reverse the first sounds in each syllable of *necktie*. (tecknie)
-Move the last syllable to the first syllable in *octagon*. (gonocta)
-Delete the last syllable in *gonocta*. (gonoct)
-Delete the last syllable in *gonoct*. (gon)
-Add *dola* to the end of *gon*. (gondola)

Use Elkonin boxes and have the student do the following:
      -Use chips to show the sounds in *neck*. (3)
       -Delete the /n/ in *neck*. (eck)
       -Change the /ĕ/ in *eck* to /ĭ/. (ick)
       -Add *pan* to the beginning of *ic*. (panic)
       -Reverse the syllables in *panic*. (icpan)
Part II

**Sound Deletion**
Say *complete* without the /l/. (compete)
Say *brake* without the /r/. (bake)
Say brands without the /r/. (bands)
Say *child* without the /l/. (chide)
Say *quilt* without the /l/. (quit)

**Segmenting Initial Sounds in Words**
What's the first sound in *prehistoric*? (/p/)
What's the first sound in *sprout*? (/s/)
What's the first sound in *traffic*? (/t/)

# Activity Twenty-Five***

Warm-up

**Directions: Show the student the following three pictures.**

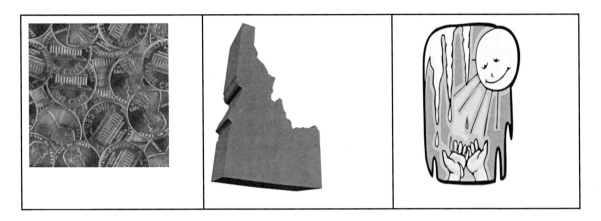

Ask: Look at the pictures. (penny, Idaho, icicle)
-How many syllables are in each of these words? (2, 3, 3)
-What is the first vowel sound you hear in each word? (/ĕ/, /ī ,/ī/)
-Put the last syllable first in *Idaho*. (ho-ida)
-Say *icicle*. Instead of *ice*, say *ora*. (oracle)
-Find a word that rhymes with *penny.*

Use Elkonin boxes and have the student do the following:
    -Use chips to show the sounds in *penny*. (4)
    -Delete the /ē/ in penny. (pen)
    -Add *cil* to the end of *pen*. (pencil)
    -Reverse the syllables in *pencil*. (silpen)
    -Change the *pen* in *silpen* to *ver*. (silver)

Part II

**Word Generation**
Think of a word that ends with /l/.
Think of a word that ends with /th/.
Think of a word that ends with /j/.
Think of a word that ends with /n/.
Think of a word that ends with /b/.

**Sound Isolation**
What sound do you hear in *quiet* that's missing in *quite*. (/ĕ/)
What sound do you hear in *mortal* that's missing in *moral*? (/t/)
What sound do you hear in *slash* that's missing *sash*? (/l/)

# Activity Twenty-Six***

Warm-up

**Directions: Show the student the following three pictures.**

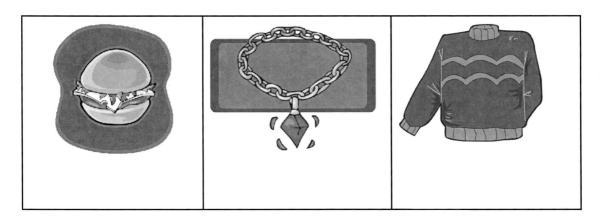

Ask: Look at the pictures. (sandwich, necklace, sweater)
-Reverse the syllables in *sandwich*. (wichsand)
-Change *sand* in *wichsand* to *hunt*. (witchhunt)
-What digraph do you hear at the end of *sandwich*? (/ch/)
-How many syllables are in each word? (2, 2, 2)
-Give a word that rhymes with *sand*.

Use Elkonin boxes and have the student do the following:
    -Use chips to show the sounds in *shirt*. (3)
    -Change the /sh/ in *shirt* to /k/. (curt)
    -Delete the /t/ in *curt*. (cur)
    -Add *tail* to the end of *cur*. (curtail)
    -Change the *cur* in *curtail* to *cotton*. (cottontail)

Part II

**Sound Substitution**
Say *clatter*. Instead of /ă/, say /ŭ/. (clutter)
Say *worthless*. Instead of /th/, say /d/. (wordless)
Say *farther*. Instead of /th/, say /m/. (farmer)
Say *snoopy*. Instead of /p/, say /t/. (snooty)
Say *statewide*. Instead of /w/, say /s/. (stateside)

**Syllable Deletion**
Say *reproduce* without *pro*. (reduce)
Say *introduce* without *tro*. (induce)
Say *cornerstone* without *ner*. (cornstone)

# Activity Twenty-Seven***

Warm-up

**Directions: Show the student the following three pictures.**

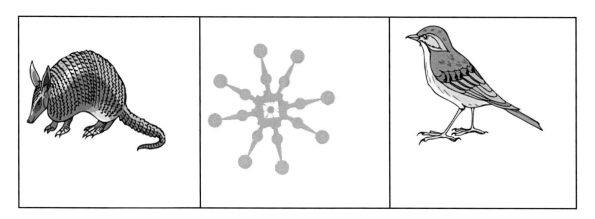

Ask: Look at the pictures. (armadillo, snowflake, swallow)
-What two words have the same ending sound? (armadillo, swallow-/ō/)
-What blends do you hear at the beginning of *snowflake* and *swallow*? (/sn/, /sw/)
-How many syllables are in each of these words? (4, 2, 2)
-Reverse the syllables in *snowflake*. (flake snow)
-Give two words that rhyme with *snow*.

Use Elkonin boxes and have the student do the following:
    -Use chips to show the sounds in *flake*. (4)
    -Delete the /l/ in *flake*. (fake)
    -Change the /k/ in fake to /m/. (fame)
    -Add /l/ after the /f/ in *fame*. (flame)
    -Add *thrower* to the end of *flame*. (flamethrower)

Part II

**Syllable Substitution**
Say *navy*. Instead of *nay*, say *way*. (wavy)
Say *meantime*. Instead of *time* say *while*. (meanwhile)
Say *kidnap*. Instead of *nap*, say *proof*. (kidproof)
Say *iceberg*. Instead of *berg*, say *cube*. (icecube)
Say *butterfly*. Instead of *fly,* say *dish*. (butterdish)

**Segmenting Initial Sounds in Words**
What's the first sound in *traffic*? (/t/)
What's the first sound in *stream*? (/s/)
What's the first sound in *grateful*? (/g/)

# Activity Twenty-Eight***

Warm-up

**Directions: Show the student the following three pictures.**

Ask: Look at the pictures. (headlight, groom, scream)
-What two words have the same ending sound? (groom, scream-/m/)
-What blends do you hear at the beginning of *groom* and *scream*? (/gr/, /scr/)
-Reverse the syllables in *headlight*. (lighthead)
-Give a word that rhymes with *groom.*

Use Elkonin boxes and have the student do the following:
    -Use chips to show the sounds in *groom.* (4)
    -Delete the /g/ in *groom.* (room)
    -Change the /m/ in *room* to /t/. (root)
    -Add *er* to the end of *root.* (rooter)

Part II

**Supplying Final Sounds in Words.**

| | |
|---|---|
| What sound do you hear in *size* that's missing in *sigh*? | (/z/) |
| What sound do you hear in *Billy* that's missing in *bill*? | (/ē/) |
| What sound do you hear in *meal* that's missing in *me*? | (/l/) |
| What sound do you hear in *maid* that's missing in *may*? | (/d/) |
| What sound do you hear in *stage* that's missing in *stay*? | (/j/) |
| What sound do you hear in *sprout* that's missing in *sprou*? | (/t/) |

**Sound Substitution**
Say *rose*. Instead of /z/, say /p/. (rope)
Say *hinge*. Instead of /j/, say /t/. (hint)
Say *jelly*. Instead of /ē/ say /ō/. (jello)
Say *heart*. Instead of /t/, say /p/. (harp)

# Activity Twenty-Nine***

Warm-up

**Directions: Show the student the following three pictures.**

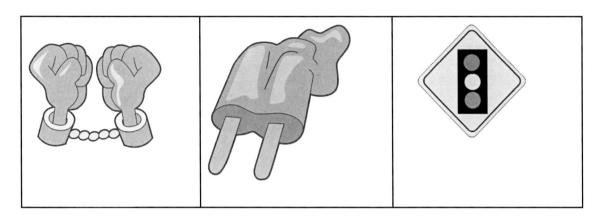

Ask: Look at the pictures. (handcuff, melt, stoplight)
-Which two words have the same ending sound? (melt, stoplight-/t/)
-How many syllables are in each word? (2,1,2)
-Reverse the syllables in *stoplight*. (lightstop)
-Change the *stop* in *lightstop* to *ning*. (lightning)
-Say *handcuff* without *hand*. (cuff)
-Give a word that rhymes with *cuff*.

Use Elkonin boxes and have the student do the following:
    -Use chips to show the sounds in *melt*. (4)
    -Delete the /t/ in *melt*. (mell)
    -Change the /e/ in *mell* to /ĭ/. (mill)
    -Add *saw* to the beginning of *mill*. (sawmill)

Part II

**Sound Substitution**
Say *sketch*. Instead of /ĕ/, say /ĭ/. (skitch)
Say *joint*. Instead of /t/, say /z/. (joins)
Say *spike*. Instead of /k/ say /t/. (spite)
Say *bland*. Instead of /l/ say /r/. (brand)
Say *style*. Instead of /ī/, say /ā/. (stale)

**Syllable Substitution**
Say *hamster*. Instead of *ham*, say *road*. (roadster)
Say *repel*. Instead of *pell*, say *fund*. (refund)
Say *rotate*. Instead of *ro*, say *mu*. (mutate)

# Activity Thirty***

Warm-up

**Directions: Show the student the following three pictures.**

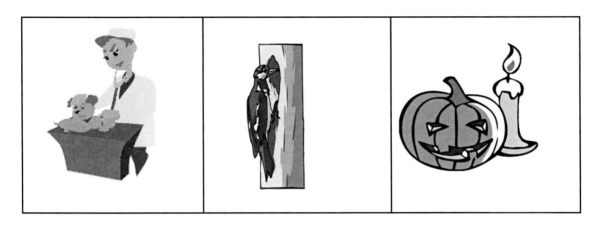

Ask: Look at the pictures. (veterinarian, woodpecker, jack-o-lantern)
-What two words have the same ending sound? (veterinarian, jack-o-lantern-/n/)
-What word has the least syllables? (woodpecker-3)
-Say *jack-o-lantern* without /ō/. (jacklantern)
-Reverse the first and last syllables in *jacklantern*. (ternlanjack)
-Delete the *ternlan* in *ternlanjack*. (jack)
-Add *car* to the beginning of *jack*. (carjack)

Use Elkonin boxes and have the student do the following:
    -Use chips to show the syllables in *woodpecker*. (3)
    -Delete the /er/ in *woodpecker*. (woodpeck)
    -Delete *wood* in *woodpeck*. (peck)
    -Change the /ĕ/ to /ĭ/ in *peck*. (pick)
    -Add *pocket* to the end of *pick*. (pickpocket)

Part II

**Phoneme Switch**
Reverse the first sounds in each word in the following:
*goldfish* (foldgish)
*jumper cable* (cumper jable)
*mail carrier* (cail marrier)

**Initial Sound Substitution**
Say *perish*. Instead of /p/ say /ch/. (cherish)
Say *round*. Instead of /r/ say /p/. (pound)
Say *pray*. Instead of /p/ say /g/. (gray)

# Activity Thirty-One***

Warm-up

**Directions: Show the student the following three pictures.**

Ask: Look at the pictures. (sneeze, bicycle, wrestle)
-Which two words have the same ending sound? (bicycle, wrestle-/l/)
-What word has the most syllables? (bicycle-3)
-What blend is at the beginning of *sneeze*? (/sn/)
-Change the /s/ in *wrestle* to /b/. (rebel)
-Reverse the syllables in *rebel*. (elreb)

Use Elkonin boxes and have the student do the following:
    -Use chips to show the sounds in *sneeze*. (4)
    -Delete the /n/ in *sneeze*. (seize)
    -Change the /z/ in *seize* to /l/. (seal)
    -Add *con* to the beginning of *seal*. (conceal)
    -Change the /s/ in *conceal* to /j/. (congeal)
    -Reverse the syllables in *congeal*. (gealcon)

Part II

**Syllable Substitution.**
Say *capture*. Instead of *cap*, say *crē*. (creature)
Say *roadster*. Instead of *road*, say *young*. (youngster)
Say *creator*. Instead of *crē*, say *cure*. (curator)
Say *flatter*. Instead of *flat*, say *pot*. (potter)
Say *beautiful*. Instead of *bū*, say *boun*. (bountiful)

**Final Sound Generation**
Think of a word that ends with /s/.
Think of a word that ends with /z/.
Think of a word that ends with /th/.

# Activity Thirty-Two***

Warm-up

**Directions: Show the student the following three pictures.**

Ask: Look at the pictures. (wristwatch, penguin, fireman)
-Which two words have the same ending sound? (penguin, fireman-/n/)
-How many syllables are in each of the words? (2)
-Switch the syllables in *fireman*. (manfire)
-Reverse the first sound in each syllable in *manfire*. (fanmire)
-Change the *man* in *fanmire* to *ad*. (admire)

Use Elkonin boxes and have the student do the following:
    -Use chips to show the sounds in *wrist*. (4)
    -Delete the /s/ in *wrist*. (writ)
    -Change the /ĭ/ in *writ* to /ī/. (write)
    -Add *copy* to the beginning of *write*. (copyright)
    -Switch the words in *copyright*. (rightcopy)
    -Instead of *right* say *photo*. (photocopy)

Part II

**Sound Substitution**
Say *bashful*. Instead of /sh/, say /th/. (bathful)
Say *telephone*. Instead of /f/, say /m/. (telemone)
Say *tattoo*. Instead of /t/, say /b/. (taboo)
Say *swoop*. Instead of /w/, say /t/. (stoop)
Say *sprain*. Instead of /p/, say /t/. (strain)

**Sound Deletion**
Say *grain* without the /r/. (gain)
Say *gloomy* without the /m/. (gluey)

# Activity Thirty-Three***

Warm-up

**Directions: Show the student the following three pictures.**

Ask: Look at the pictures. (finger, fireplace, highchair)
-Which two words have the same ending sound? (finger, highchair-/r/)
-Which two words have the same beginning sound? (finger, fireplace-/f/)
-How many syllables are in each of the words? (2)
-Say *fireplace* without *fire*. (place)
-Add *ment* to the end of *place*. (placement)
-Find two words that rhyme with *chair*.

Use Elkonin boxes and have the student do the following:
    -Use chips to show the sounds in *place*. (4)
    -Change the /s/ in *place* to /t/. (plate)
    -Change the /ā/ in *plate* to /ē/. (pleat)
    -Add *com* to the beginning of *pleat*. (complete)
    -Change *plete* in *complete* to *cast*. (comcast)

Part II

**Blend Generation**
Think of a word that begins with the blend /scr/.
Think of a word that begins with the blend /pr/.
Think of a word that begins with the blend /gr/.
Think of a word that begins with the blend /tr/.
Think of a word that begins with the blend /fr/.

**Syllable Addition**
Add *ket* to the end of *gas*. (gasket)
Add *cast* to the end of *type*. (typecast)
Add *fume* to the end of *per*. (perfume)

# Activity Thirty-Four***

Warm-up

**Directions: Show the student the following three pictures.**

Ask: Look at the pictures. (flip-flop, faucet, filmstrip)
-Which two words have the same ending sound? (filmstrip, flip-flop-/f/)
-How many syllables are in each word? (2)
-What word begins with a blend? (flip-flop-/fl/)
-Switch the syllables in *flip flop*. (flopflip)
-Change the *flip* in *flop flip* to *house*. (flophouse)

Use Elkonin boxes and have the student do the following:
    -Use chips to show the syllables in *filmstrip*. (2)
    -Delete *film* in *filmstrip*. (strip)
    -Use chips to show the sounds in *strip*. (5)
    -Change the /ĭ/ in *strip* to /ī/. (stripe)
    -Change the /p/ in *stripe* to /d/. (stride)

Part II

**Identifying Missing Sounds in Words**
What sound do you hear in *exist* that's missing in *exit*? (/s/)
What sound do you hear in *frail* that's missing in *fail*? (/r/)
What sound do you hear in *homely* that's missing in *holy*? (/m/)
What sound do you hear in *middle* that's missing in *mill*? (/d/)
What sound do you hear in *charge* that's missing in *char*? (/j/)

**Segmenting Syllables in Words**
How many syllables are in *entertain*? (3)
How many syllables are in *topiary*? (4)
How many syllables are in *infirmary*? (4)

# Activity Thirty-Five***

Warm-up

**Directions: Show the student the following three pictures.**

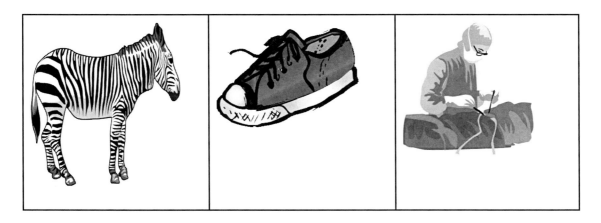

Ask: Look at the pictures. (zebra, sneaker, doctor)
-Which two words have the same ending sound? (sneaker, doctor-/er/)
-How many syllables are in each word? (2)
-Which word has a blend at the beginning? What is the blend? (sneaker-/sn/)
-Which words have a long vowel sound in them? (zebra, sneaker-/ee/)
-Say *sneaker* without *er*. (sneak)
-Find two words that rhyme with *sneak*.

Use Elkonin boxes and have the student do the following:
  -Use chips to show the syllables in *zebra*. (2)
  -Delete the *brah* in *zebra*. (zee)
  -Add *nith* to the end of *zee*. (zenith)
  -Change the /ē/ in *zenith* to /oo/. (zoonith)
  -Delete the *ith* in *zoonith*. (zoon)
  -Change the /z/ in *zoon* to /s/. (soon)

Part II

**Phoneme Substitution**
Say *cortex*. Instead of /k/, say /v/. (vortex)
Say *flabby*. Instead of /b/, say /sh/. (flashy)
Say *spender*. Instead of /p/, say /l/. (slender)
Say *left*. Instead of /f/, say /s/. (lest)
Say *hockey*. Instead of /k/, say /b/. (hobby)

**Syllable Deletion**
Say *termite* without *mite*. (ter)
Say *hairdryer* without *dry*. (hairer)

# Activity Thirty-Six***

Warm-up

**Directions: Show the student the following three pictures.**

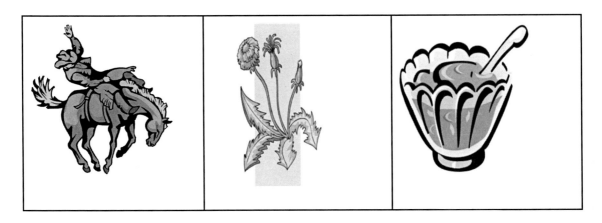

Ask: Look at the pictures. (bronco, dandelion, gelatin)
-Which two words have the same ending sound? (dandelion, gelatin-/n/)
-How many syllables are in each word? (2, 4, 3)
-Change the /ō/ in bronco to /ī/. (bronchi)
-Add *tis* to the end of *bronchi*. (bronchitis)
-Give a word that rhymes with *dandy*.

Use Elkonin boxes and have the student do the following:
    -Use chips to show the syllables in *gelatin*. (3)
    -Take the last syllable in *gelatin* and put it first. (tingela)
    -Take off *gela* and add *sel* to the end. (tinsel)
    -Replace the *tin* with *dam*. (damsel)
    -Change the /d/ in *damsel* to /l/. (lamsel)

Part II

**Hidden Syllables**
Is the syllable *sist* in these words?
persist? (y)
sister? (y)
traitor? (n)
resistant? (y)
protract? (n)

**Syllable Reversal**
Reverse the syllables in *coon-tie*. (tycoon)
Reverse the syllables in *castfor*. (forecast)
Reverse the syllables in *poison*. (zunpoi)

# Activity Thirty-Seven***

Warm-up

**Directions: Show the student the following three pictures.**

Ask: Look at the pictures. (watercolors, humpback whale, ferris wheel)
-Which two words have the same ending sound? (humpback whale, ferris wheel)
-How many syllables are in each word? (4, 3, 3)
-Reverse the syllables in *ferris wheel*. (wheel ferris).
-Reverse the first sounds in each syllable of *wheel ferris*. (feel wherris)
-Change *wherris* in *feelwherris* to /er/. (feeler)
-Give a word that rhymes with *whale.*

Use Elkonin boxes and have the student do the following:
    -Use chips to show the syllables in *watercolor*. (4)
    -Switch the words in *water color*. (colorwater)
    -Delete *color* from *water color*. (water)
    -Use chips to show the sounds in *water*. (4)
    -Change the /w/ in *water* to /l/. (lotter)
    -Add /b/ to the beginning of *lotter*. (blotter)

Part II

**Rhyme Generation**
Give three words that rhyme with *stove*.
Give three words that rhyme with *pile*.
Give three words that rhyme with *board*.
Give three words that rhyme with *caught*.
Give three words that rhyme with *crown*.

**Final Consonant Isolation**
Think of a word that doesn't rhyme with, but has the same last sound as *slosh*.
Think of a word that doesn't rhyme with, but has the same last sound as *judgment*.

# Activity Thirty-Eight***

Warm-up

**Directions: Show the student the following three pictures.**

Ask: Look at the pictures. (giant, dentist, football)
-What two words have the same ending sound? (giant, dentist-/t/)
-How many syllables are in each word? (2)
-Reverse the syllables in *dentist*. (tistden)
-Reverse the first sounds in each syllable of *football*. (bootfall)
-Change the /b/ in *bootfall* to /s/. (sootfall)
-Give two words that rhyme with *fall*.

Use Elkonin boxes and have the student do the following:
    -Use chips to show the syllables in *giant*. (2)
    -Add /g/ after the /ī/ in giant. (gigant)
    -Add *ic* to the end of *gigant*. (gigantic)
    -Delete the jī in gigantic. (gantic)
    -Change the /g/ in *gantic* to /r/. (rantic)
    -Add /f/ to the beginning of *rantic*. (frantic)

Part II

**Phoneme Deletion**
Say *flask* without the /s/. (flack)
Say *probe* without the /b/. (pro)
Say *clove* without the /l/. (cove)
Say *smell* without the /m/. (sell)
Say *trend* without the /r/. (tend)

**Sound Isolation**
What sound do you hear in *spank* that's missing in *sank*? (/p/)
What sound do you hear in *playtime* that's missing in *paytime*? (/l/)

# Activity Thirty-Nine***

Warm-up

**Directions: Show the student the following three pictures.**

Ask: Look at the pictures. (slice, prince, gymnast)
-What two words have the same ending sound? (slice, prince-/s/)
-How many syllables are in each word? (1, 1, 2)
-Reverse the syllables in *gymnast*. (nastgym)
-Delete the last syllable from *nastgym*. (nast)
-Add /ē/ to the end of *nast*. (nasty)
-Give a word that rhymes with *slice*.

Use Elkonin boxes and have the student do the following:
  -Use chips to show the sounds in *prince*. (5)
  -Change the /s/ in *prince* to /t/. (print)
  -Delete the /r/ in *print*. (pĭnt)
  -Change the /ĭ/ in *pint* to /oi/. (point)
  -Add *blank* to the end of *point*. (pointblank)

Part II

**Syllable Substitution**
Say *wintry*. Instead of *tree,* say *ter.* (winter)
Say *zealous.* Instead of *zeal*, say *fame.* (famous)
Say *decorator.* Instead of *decorate*, say *illustrate.* (illustrator)
Say *leisure.* Instead of *leezh,* say *plezh.* (pleasure)
Say *classical.* Instead of *class*, say *trop.* (tropical)

**Segmenting Syllables in Words**
How many syllables are in *vehicle*? (3)
How many syllables are in *retch*? (1)
How many syllables are in *tabernacle*? (4)

# Activity Forty***

Warm-up

**Directions: Show the student the following three pictures.**

Ask: Look at the pictures. (pottery, raspberry, giraffe)
-Which two words have the same ending sound? (pottery, raspberry-/ee/)
-How many syllables are in each word? (3, 3, 2)
-Say *giraffe* without *af*. (jer)
-Add *nee* to the end of *jer*. (journey)
-Say *pottery* without *er*. (potty)
-Give a word that rhymes with *berry*.

Use Elkonin boxes and have the student do the following:
    -Use chips to show the sounds in *potty*. (4)
    -Change the /o/ in *potty* to /i/. (pity)
    -Add /r/ after the /p/ in *pity*. (pretty)
    -Change the /t/ in *pretty* to /s/. (prissy)
    -Delete the /ee/ in *prissy*. (priss)
    -Add *teen* to the end of *priss*. (pristine)

Part II

**Sound Isolation**
What sound do you hear in *mortal* that's missing in *moral*? (/t/)
What sound do you hear in *tidal* that's missing in *tile*. (/d/)
What sound do you hear in *radon* that's missing in *rayon*? (/d/)
What sound do you hear in *monkey* that's missing in *money*? (/k/)

**Syllable Addition**
Add *ward* to the end of *west*. (westward)
Add *board* to the end of *spring*. (springboard)
Add *chur* to the end of *tor*. (torture)

# Activity Forty-One***

Warm-up

**Directions: Show the student the following three pictures.**

Ask: Look at the pictures. (gypsy, genie, brownie)
-What two words have the same ending sound? (genie, brownie-/ee/)
-What two words have the same beginning sound? (genie, gypsy-/j/)
-How many syllables are in each word? (2)
-Say *gypsy* without *see*. (gyp)
-Replace the /p/ with /k/. (gic)
-Add *tră* to the beginning of *gic*. (tragic)
-Give a word that rhymes with *brown*.

Use Elkonin boxes and have the student do the following:
    -Use chips to show the sounds in *genie*. (4)
    -Delete the /nē/ and add /p/. (jeep)
    -Change the /j/ in jeep to /l/. (leap)
    -Add /s/ to the beginning of *leap*. (sleep)
    -Add *walk* to the end of *sleep*. sleepwalk)

Part II

**Syllable Reversal**
Reverse the syllables in *gumdrop*. (dropgum)
Reverse the syllables in *perceive*. (seevper)
Reverse the syllables in *keywhis*. (whiskey)
Reverse the syllables in *recline*. (cline-re)

**Syllable Substitution**
Say *involve*. Instead of *in*, say /ē/. (evolve)
Say *party*. Instead of *ty*, say *snip*. (parsnip)
Say *pantry*. Instead of *pan*, say *cun*. (country)

# Activity Forty-Two***

Warm-up

**Directions: Show the student the following three pictures.**

Ask: Look at the pictures. (scoreboard, braces, gingerbread)
-What two words have the same ending sound? (scoreboard, gingerbread-/d/)
-How many syllables are in each word? (2, 2, 3)
-Which words have blends in them? (scoreboard-/sc/, braces-/br/)
-Say *gingerbread* without *bread*. (ginger)
-Change the *gin* in *ginger* to *plun*. (plunger)
-Give three words that rhyme with *score*.

Use Elkonin boxes and have the student do the following:
    -Use chips to show the sounds in *brace*. (4)
    -Change the /s/ in *brace* to /d/. (braid)
    -Change the /r/ in *braid* to /l/. (blade)
    -Add *switch* to the beginning of *blade*. (switchblade)

Part II

**Sound Isolation**
What sound do you hear in *white* that's missing in *why*? (/t/)
What sound do you hear in *roast* that's missing in *wrote*? (/s/)
What sound do you hear in *drove* that's missing in *dove*? (/r/)
What sound do you hear in *child* that's missing in *chide*? (/l/)
What sound do you hear in *went* that's missing in *wet*? (/n/)

**Rhyme Generation**
Think of three words that rhyme with *style*.
Think of three words that rhyme with *coast*.
Think of three words that rhyme with *latch*.

# Activity Forty-Three***

Warm-up

**Directions: Show the student the following three pictures.**

Ask: Look at the pictures. (refrigerator, cactus, cheerleader)
-What two words have the same ending sound? (refrigerator, cheerleader-/r/)
-How many syllables are in each word? (5, 2, 3)
-Which word begins with a digraph? (cheerleader-/ch/)
-Say *refrigerator* without *re*. (frigerator)
-Take off the first *er* in *frigerator*. (frijator)
-Give a word that rhymes with *whale*.

Use Elkonin boxes and have the student do the following:
    -Use chips to show the syllables in *cactus*. (2)
    -Take off the last syllable in *cactus*. (cac)
    -Add /t/ to the end of *cac*. (cact)
    -Change the first sound in *cact* to /p/. (pact)
    -Add *com* to the beginning of *pact*. (compact)

Part II

**Syllable Substitution (Nonsense Words)**
Say *explanation*. Instead of *plan*, say *trim*. (extrimation)
Say *wonderful*. Instead of *der*, say *stip*. (wonstipful)
Say *dangerous*. Instead of *jer*, say *bif*. (danbifous)
Say *convertible*, Instead of *vert*, say *moot*. (conmootible)
Say *information*. Instead of *ma*, say *go*. (inforgotion)

**Vowel Discrimination**
Think of a word that has the same vowel sound as *spent*.
Think of a word that has the same vowel sound as *mint*.
Think of a word that has the same vowel sound as *gloom*.

# Activity Forty-Four***

Warm-up

**Directions: Show the student the following three pictures.**

Ask: Look at the pictures. (banana, school bus, sawhorse)
-What two words have the same ending sound? (school bus, sawhorse-/s/)
-How many syllables are in each word? (3, 2, 2)
-Reverse the syllables in *school bus*. (bus school)
-Say *sawhorse* without the *saw*. (horse)
-Add *fly* to the end of *horse*. (horsefly)
-Give a word that rhymes with *horse*.

Use Elkonin boxes and have the student do the following:
 -Use chips to show the sounds in *bus*. (3)
 -Change the /b/ in *bus* to /m/. (mus)
 -Add /t/ to the end of *mus*. (must)
 -Change the /m/ in *must* to /r/. (rust)
 -Add /k/ to the beginning of *rust*. (crust)

Part II

**Sound Segmentation**
Tap out the sounds in *stretch*. (/s/ /t/ /r/ /e/ /ch/)
Tap out the sounds in *flask*. (/f/ /l/ /a/ /s/ /k/)
Tap out the sounds in *scrunch*. (/s/ /k/ /r/ /u/ /n/ /ch/)
Tap out the sounds in *strict*. (/s/ /t/ /r/ /i/ /k/ /t/)

**Syllable Reversal**
Reverse the syllables in *dosage*. (ijdose)
Reverse the syllables in *earthling*. (lingearth)
Reverse the syllables in *pearly*. (lypearl)

# Activity Forty-Five***

Warm-up

**Directions: Show the student the following three pictures.**

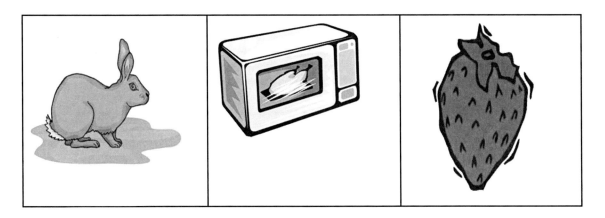

Ask: Look at the pictures. (bunny, microwave, strawberry)
-What two words have the same ending sound? (bunny, strawberry-/ee/)
-Which word has a blend at the beginning? (strawberry-/str/)
-How many syllables are in each word? (2, 3, 3)
-Say *microwave* without *crō*. (miwave)
-Say *strawberry* without *straw*. (berry)
-Give a word that rhymes with *bunny*.

Use Elkonin boxes and have the student do the following:
    -Use chips to show the sounds in *straw*. (4)
    -Delete the /r/ in *straw*. (staw)
    -Change the /t/ in *staw* to /l/. (slaw)
    -Add /n/ to the end of *slaw*. (slawn)
    -Add /t/ to the end of *slawn*. (slawnt)
    -Replace the /aw/ in slawnt with /ă/. (slant)

Part II

**Sound Substitution**
Say *least*. Instead of /s/, say /f/. (leafed)
Say *spared*. Instead of /p/, say /k/. (scared)
Say *spunk*. Instead of /p/, say /l/. (slunk)
Say *grave*. Instead of /v/ say /p/. (grape)

**Segmenting Syllables in Words**
How many syllables are in *blackboard*. (2)
How many syllables are in *redesign*. (3)

# Activity Forty-Six***

Warm-up

**Directions: Show the student the following three pictures.**

Ask: Look at the pictures. (desert, grapefruit, jumprope)
-Which two words have the same ending sound? (desert, grapefruit-/t/)
-How many syllables are in each word? (2, 2, 2)
-Reverse the syllables in *grapefruit.* (fruitgrape)
-Say *desert* without *dez.* (ert)
-Add *Herb* to the beginning of *ert.* (Herbert)
-Give a word that rhymes with *jump.*

Use Elkonin boxes and have the student do the following:
    -Use chips to show the sounds in *rope.* (3)
    -Change the /ō/ in *rope* to /ī/. (ripe)
    -Add /g/ to the beginning of *ripe.* (gripe)
    -Change the /p/ in *gripe* to /n/. (grine)
    -Add /d/ to the end of *grine.* (grind)

**Part II**

**Sound Isolation**
What sound do you hear in *fable* that's missing in *fail*? (/b/)
What sound do you hear in *splashed* that's missing in *slashed*? (/p/)
What sound do you hear in *scuffle* that's missing in *scuff*? (/l/)
What sound do you hear in *slurp* that's missing in *slur*? (/p/)
What sound do you hear in *stain* that's missing in *sane.* (/t/)

**Initial Sound Deletion (some nonsense words)**
Say *curdle* without the /k/. (urdle)
Say *sturdy* without the /s/. (turdy)
Say *lawful* without the /l/. (awful)
Say *scrawl* without the /s/. (crawl)

# Activity Forty-Seven***

Warm-up

**Directions: Show the student the following three pictures.**

Ask: Look at the pictures. (diamond ring, icing, dragon)
-What two words have the same ending sound? (diamond ring, icing-/ng/))
-How many syllables are in each word? (3, 2, 2)
-What two words have a long vowel sound in them? (diamond ring, icing-/i-e/)
-What word has a blend in it? What is it? (dragon-/dr/)
-Say *dragon* without the *on*. (drag)
-Give two words that rhyme with *drag*.

Use Elkonin boxes and have the student do the following:
    -Use chips to show the syllables in *icing*. (2)
    -Add /r/ to the beginning of *icing*. (ricing)
    -Add /p/ to the beginning of *ricing*. (pricing)
    -Delete the *ing* in *pricing*. (price)
    -Add *tag* to the end of *price*. (pricetag)

Part II

**Rhyme Identification**
Which word rhymes with *spoon*?    spoof    groom    tune    (tune)
Which word rhymes with *blast*?    staff    last    strap    (last)
Which word rhymes with *toast*?    roast    hope    gloat    (roast)
Which word rhymes with *gain*?    laid    brain    tape    (brain)
Which word rhymes with *stroll*?    poke    host    goal    (goal)

**Phoneme Addition**
Add /v/ to the end of *cur*. (curve)
Add /j/ to the end of *char*. (charge)

# Activity Forty-Eight***

Warm-up

**Directions: Show the student the following three pictures.**

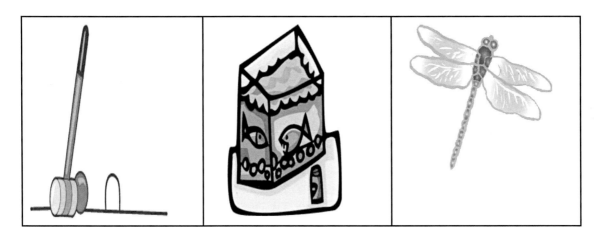

Ask: Look at the pictures. (croquet, aquarium, dragonfly)
-What two words have a blend at the beginning? (croquet-/cr/, dragonfly-/dr/)
-How many syllables are in each word? (2, 4, 3)
-Say *dragonfly* without *on*. (dragfly)
-Say *croquet* without *kay*. (krō)
-Add /m/ to the end of *kro*. (chrome)

Use Elkonin boxes and have the student do the following:
    -Use chips to show the sounds in *drag*. (4)
    -Change the /g/ in *drag* to /p/. (drap)
    -Change the /a/ in *drap* to /ā/. (drape)
    -Add *er* to the end of *drape*. (draper)
    -Add /ē/ to the end of *draper*. (drapery)

Part II

**Phoneme Blending**
Talk like a robot and have students blend these phonemes.
/s/ /k/ /i/ /m/ /p/        (skimp)
/k/ /r/ /e/ /s/ /t/         (crest)
/b/ /r/ /u/ /n/ /ch/       (brunch)
/t/ /r/ /e/ /n/ /ch/       (trench)

**Phoneme Generation**
Think of a word that has the same last sound as *graceful.*
Think of a word that has the same last sound as *smith.*
Think of a word that has the same last sound as *fluff.*

# Activity Forty-Nine***

Warm-up

**Directions: Show the student the following three pictures**

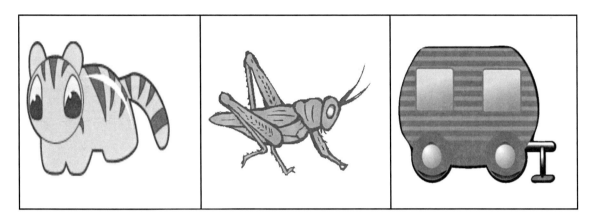

Ask: Look at the pictures. (ocelot, cricket, trailer)
-What two words have the same ending sound? (ocelot, cricket-/t/)
-How many syllables are in each word? (3, 2, 2)
-Which two words have a blend in them? (cricket-/cr/, trailer-/tr/)
-Delete the /ŭ/ in *ocelot*. (oslot)
-Add /k/ to the beginning of *oslot*. (koslot)
-Add /t/ after the /s/ in *coslot*. (costlot)
-Give a word that rhymes with *cost*.

Use Elkonin boxes and have the student do the following:
    -Use chips to show the sounds in *crick*. (4)
    -Change the /r/ in *crick* to /l/. (click)
    -Take off the last sound in *click* and put in /p/. (clip)
    -Change the /ĭ/ in *clip* to /ă/. (clap)
    -Add /s/ after the /a/ in *clap*. (clasp)

Part II

**Syllable Reversal.**
Reverse the syllables in *postpone*. (ponepost)
Reverse the syllables in *Neptune*. (tunenep)
Reverse the syllables in *dateline*. (linedate)
Reverse the syllables in *waistline*. (linewaist)
Reverse the syllables in *discharge*. (chargedis)

**Final Sound Deletion**
What sound do you hear in *gnome* that's missing in *no*. (/m/)
What sound do you hear in *rhyme* that's missing in *rye*? (/m/)

# Activity Fifty***

Warm-up

**Directions: Show the student the following three pictures.**

Ask: Look at the pictures. (lawnmower, invitation, dinosaur)
-Which two words have the same ending sound? (lawn mower, dinosaur-/r/)
-How many syllables are in each word? (3, 4, 3)
-Which word begins with a vowel sound? What is it? (invitation-/i/)
-Say *lawnmower* without *er*. (lawnmow)
-Reverse the syllables in *lawnmow*. (mowlawn)
-Give a word that rhymes with *mow*.

Use Elkonin boxes and have the student do the following:
    -Use chips to show the sounds in *lawn*. (3)
    -Change the /n/ in *lawn* to /d/. (laud)
    -Add /s/ after the vowel sound in *lot*. (lost)
    -Change the /o/ in *lost* to /ō/. (loast)
    -Change the /l/ in loast to /b/. (boast)

Part II

**Syllable Substitution**
Say *admit*. Instead of *mit*, say *ress*. (address)
Say *western*. Instead of *west*, say *north*. (northern)
Say *propose*. Instead of *pro*, say *com*. (compose)
Say *fluster*. Instead of *flus*, say *can*. (canter)

**Phoneme Deletion**
Say *brute* without the /r/. (boot)
Say *grape* without the /r/. (gape)
Say *grill* without the /r/. (gill)
Say *munch* without the /n/. (much)

# Level Three Activities

# Activity One*****

Warm-up

**Directions: Show the student the following three pictures.**

Ask: Look at the pictures. (windmill, hamburger, jack-in-the-box)
-Which word has the most syllables? How many? (jack-in-the-box-4)
-Say *hamburger* without the second syllable. (hamger)
-Take the first syllable in *hamburger* and put it last. (burgerham)
-Take the first syllable in *windmill* and the first syllable in *hamburger* and make a new word. (windham)
-Take the last syllable in *windmill* and the last syllable in *jack-in-the-box* and make a new word. (millbox)

Part II

**Syllable Deletion**
Say *complimentary* without *com*. What's left? (plimentary)
Say *admission* without *ad*. What's left? (mission)
Say *dramatize* without *tize*. What's left? (drama)
Say *membership* without *ber*. What's left? (memship)
Say *flowershop* without *er*. What's left? (flowshop)
Say *basketball* without *ket*. What's left? (basball)

**Syllable Reversal**
Reverse the syllables in *neighbor*. (borneigh)
Reverse the syllables in *hydrant*. (drant-hy)
Reverse the syllables in *youngster*. (steryoung)
Reverse the syllables in *halo*. (lo-hā)

# Activity Two*****

Warm-up

**Directions: Show the student the following three pictures.**

Ask: Look at the pictures. (piggyback, jelly beans, treasure chest)
-How many syllables are in each of the words? (3)
-What digraphs do you hear in *piggyback* and *chest*? (/ck/, /ch/)
-Reverse the syllables in *piggyback*. (backpiggy)
-Switch the first sounds in *piggypack*. (biggypack)
-Switch the first sound in each word in *jelly beans*. (bellyjeans)

Part II

**Sound Deletion**
Say *strap* without the /s/. (trap)
Say *shriek* without the /r/. (sheik)
Say *fright* without the /r/. (fight)
Say *blind* without the /l/. (bind)
Say *glisten* without the /g/. (listen)
Say *brought* without /r/. (bought)

**Pig Latin**
In Pig Latin you take off the first sound in a word and put it at the end of the word and add /ā/. Jump would be umpjay.
Say *boat* in Pig Latin. (oatbay)
Say *shirt* in Pig Latin. (irtshay)
Say *plant* in Pig Latin. (lantpay)
Say *blouse* in Pig Latin. (lousebay)
Say *tantrum* in Pig Latin. (antrumtay)
Say *buddy* in Pig Latin. (uddybay)

# Activity Three*****

Warm-up

**Directions: Show the student the following three pictures.**

Ask: Look at the pictures. (marble, waterfall, washing machine)
-How many syllables are in each word? (2, 3, 4)
-What two words have the same first vowel sound in them? (waterfall, washing machine)
-Which two words end with the same sound? (marble, waterfall-/l/)
-Reverse the words in *washing machine*. (machine washing)
-Take the first sound in each word and reverse them. (wachine moshing)
-Take the last syllable in *waterfall* and the last syllable in *washboard* and make a new word. (fallboard)

Part II

**Sound Deletion**
Say *hunch* without the /n/. (hutch)
Say *roster* without the /s/. (rotter)
Say *grand* without the /n/. (grad)
Say *table* without the /b/. (tail)
Say *sport* without the /p/. (sort)
Say *past* without the /s/. (pat)

**Phoneme Substitution**
Say *blank*. Instead of /ā/, say /i/. (blink)
Say *blister*. Instead of /i/, say /u/. (bluster)
Say *begin*. Instead of /i/, say /u/. (begun)
Say *fright*. Instead of /r/, say /l/. (flight)
Say *lent*. Instead of /n/, say /s/. (lest)
Say *stable*. Instead of /b/, say /p/. (staple)

# Activity Four*****

Warm-up

**Directions: Show the student the following three pictures.**

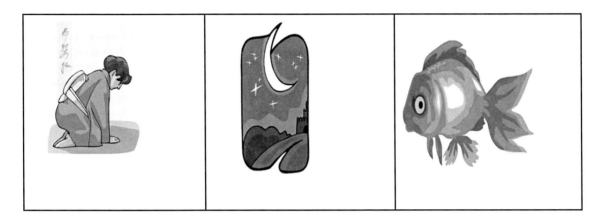

Ask: Look at the pictures. (kimono, moonlight, goldfish )
-Which word has the most syllables in it? How many? (kimono-3)
-Where is the digraph in *goldfish*? What is it? (end-/sh/)
-Say *kimono* with the first syllable last. (monoki)
-Say *moonlight*. Switch the first and last sounds in *moonlight*. (toonlime)
-Take the first syllable in each word and make a new word. (kimoongold)
-Reverse the first sound in each syllable in *goldfish*. (foldgish)

Part II

**Sound Substitution**
Say *tell*. Take off /b/ and put in /b/. (bell)
Say *pole*. Take off /l/ and put in /k/. (poke)
Say *tribe*. Take off /t/ and put in /b/. (bribe)
Say *hair*. Take off /h/ and put in /ch/. (chair)
Say *faith*. Take off /th/ and put in /s/. (face)
Say *health*. Take off /th/ and put in /p/. (help)

**Phoneme Switch**
Switch the first sounds in the words *mountain lion*. (lountain mion)
Switch the first sounds in the words *northern lights*. (lorthern nights)
Switch the first sounds in the two words *pipe line*. (lipe pine)
Switch the first sounds in the words *pin cushion*. (kin pushion)
Switch the first sounds in the words Red Sox. (Sed Rox)
Switch the first sounds in the words *polar bear*. (bolar pear)
Switch the first sounds in the words *paper towel*. (taper powel)

# Activity Five*****

Warm-up

**Directions: Show the student the following three pictures.**

Ask: Look at the pictures. (lemonade, rollerblade, lobster)
-Which two words have the same number of syllables? How many? (lemonade, rollerblade-3)
-What two words rhyme? (lemonade, rollerblade)
-Take the last syllable in *rollerblade* and the last syllable in *lobster* to make a new word. (bladester)
-Say *lemonade* without the second syllable. (lemade)
-Take the first syllable in each of the words and make a new word. (lemrolob)

Part II

**Pig Latin**
Say *charcoal* in Pig Latin. (arcoalchay)
Say *fender* in Pig Latin. (enderfay)
Say *playground* in Pig Latin. (laygroundpay)
Say *rattlesnake* in Pig Latin. (attlesnakeray)
Say *sport* in Pig Latin. (portsay)
Say *donut* in Pig Latin. (onutday)
Say *family* in Pig Latin. (amilyfay)

**Syllable Substitution**
Say *mailbox.* Instead of *mail,* say *voice.* (voicebox)
Say *landscape.* Instead of *scape,* say *fill.* (landfill)
Say *doorbell.* Instead of *bell* say *knob.* (doorknob)
Say *damage.* Instead of *ige,* say *zel.* (damsel)
Say *pizza.* Instead of *za,* say *nut.* (peanut)
Say *maximum.* Instead of *max,* say *min.* (minimum)

# Activity Six*****

Warm-up

**Directions: Show the student the following three pictures.**

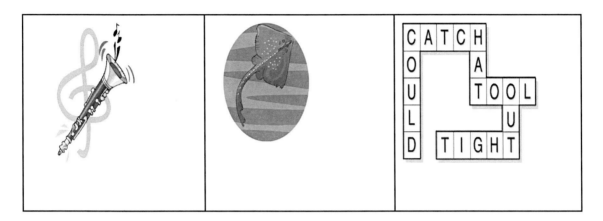

Ask: Look at the pictures. (clarinet, stingray, scrabble)
-How many syllables are in *clarinet*? (3)
-What are the blends at the beginning of each word? (/cl/, /st/, /scr/)
-Say *stingray* backwards. (raysting)
-Say *clarinet* without the second syllable. (claret)
-Say *clarinet* without the first sound. (larinet)
-Take the last syllable in *stingray* and the last syllable in *scrabble* and make a new word. (rayble)
-Now take the first syllable in *stingray* and the last syllable in *clarinet* to make a new word. (stingnet)

Part II

**Phoneme Switch**
Switch the first sounds in each syllable.
*doorway*         (woorday)
*female*          (mefale)
*homework*        (womehork)
*meanwhile*       (wheanmile)
*newscast*        (kewsnast)

**Syllable Substitution**
Say_____. Instead of _____ say_____.
   landmark         mark         fill         landfill
   dishpan          pan          towel        dishtowel
   pocket           pock         mark         market
   playground       ground       house        playhouse

# Activity Seven*****

Warm-up

**Directions: Show the student the following three pictures.**

Ask: Look at the pictures. (polar bear, Frankenstein, yogurt)
-Which pictures have the most syllables? (polar bear, Frankenstein-3)
-Switch the first sounds in each syllable of *polar bear*. (bolar pear)
-What blend do you hear at the beginning of *Frankenstein*? (/fr/)
-Take off the second syllable in *polar bear*. What's left? (pobear)
-Move the first syllable in *polar bear* to the end. (larbearpo)
-Take the last syllable in *polar bear* and the last syllable in *yogurt* and make a new word. (beargurt)
-Switch the first and last sounds in the word *polar bear*. (rolarbape)

Part II

**Sound Deletion Within Words**
Say *clamp* without the /m/. (clap)
Say *swept* without the /p/. (sweat)
Say *splint* without the /n/. (split)
Say *grist* without the /s/. (grit)
Say *task* without the /s/. (tack)
Say *steeple* without the /p/. (steel)

**Phoneme Substitution**
Say _____. Replace the ____ with _____.

| | | | |
|---|---|---|---|
| advice | /s/ | /z/ | (advise) |
| crock | /k/ | /p/ | (crop) |
| flame | /m/ | /k/ | (flake) |
| close | /z/ | /n/ | (clone) |
| spider | /p/ | /l/ | (slider) |

# Activity Eight*****

Warm-up

**Directions: Show the student the following three pictures.**

Ask: Look at the pictures. (stapler, flower, honeybee)
-What two words have the same ending sound? (stapler, flower-/r/)
-What blends do you hear at the beginning of *stapler* and *flower*? (/st/, /fl/)
-Reverse the syllables in *stapler*. (plersta)
-Switch the first sound in each word of *honeybee*. (boneyhee)
-Say *stapler*. Change the /ā/ to /i/. (stippler)
-Take the first syllable in *stapler* and the last syllable in *flower* to make a new word. (stayer)

Part II

**Phoneme Switch**
**Say the following words and switch the first sound in each word.**
*natural gas*        (gatural nas)
*physical therapy*   (thysical ferapy)
*pitchfork*          (fitchpork)
*playing card*       (claying pard)
*pocket money*       (mocket poney)
*sailboat*           (bailsoat)

**Syllable Substitution**
Say *backfire*. Instead of *back*, say *camp*. (campfire)
Say *nutmeg*. Instead of *meg*, say *shell*. (nutshell)
Say *awkward*. Instead of *ward*, say *land*. (awkland)
Say *nautical*. Instead of *cal*, say *lus*. (nautilus)
Say *overhaul*. Instead of *haul*, say *board*. (overboard)

# Activity Nine*****

Warm-up

**Directions: Show the student the following three pictures.**

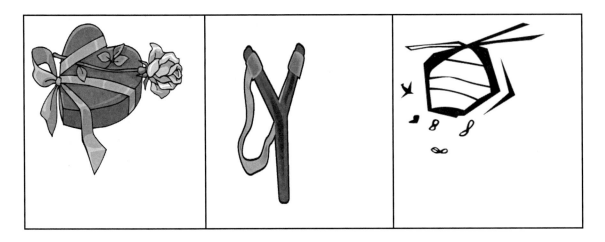

Ask: Look at the pictures. (valentine, slingshot, beehive)
-How many syllables are in each of these words? (3, 2, 2)
-Reverse the syllables in *slingshot*. (shotsling)
-Change *sling* in *shotsling* to *gun*. (shotgun)
-Reverse the first sound in each syllable of *shotgun*. (gotshun)
-Take the first syllable in *slingshot* and the last syllable in *beehive* and make a new word. (slinghive)
-Take the first syllable in each word and make a new word. (valslingbee)
-Take the first and last sound in *valentine* and switch them. (nalentive)

Part II

**Phoneme Switch**
**Say each word backwards.**
*teach*　　　(cheat)
*tale*　　　(late)
*pain*　　　(nape)
*sham*　　　(mash)
*spite*　　　(types)

**Syllable Reversal**
**Reverse the syllables in...**
*confront*　　(frontcon)
*income*　　(come-in)
*tourist*　　(isttour)
*motel*　　　(telmo)

# Activity Ten*****

Warm-up

**Directions: Show the student the following three pictures.**

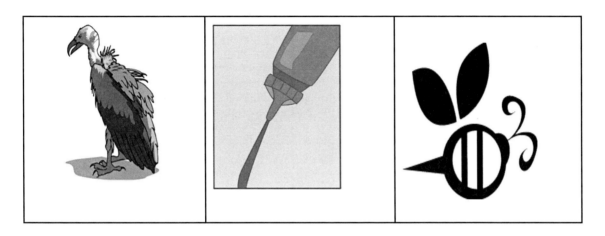

Ask: Look at the pictures. (vulture, ketchup, stinger)
-What two words have the same ending sound? (vulture, stinger-/r/)
-How many syllables does each of the words have? (2)
-Say *ketchup* backwards. (upketch)
-Change the *ketch* in *upketch* to *ward*. (upward)
-Say *vulture* without *ture*. (vul)
-Add *can* to the end of *vul*. (Vulcan)
-Take the first syllable in *vulture* and the first syllable in *stinger* and make a new word. (vulsting)

Part II

**Syllable Reversal (Use chips as necessary.)**
Switch the first and last syllables in the word:
*hypnosis*    (sisnohyp)
*barnacle*    (cle-a-barn)
*wilderness*    (nesserwild)
*September*    (bertemsep)
*penmanship*    (shipmanpen)

**Syllable Substitution**
Say *enrichment*. Instead of *rich* say *trench*. (entrenchment)
Say *dorsal*. Instead of *sal* say *mant*. (dormant)
Say *forest*. Instead of *est* say *lorn*. (forlorn)
Say *organic*. Instead of *ic* say *ize*. (organize)
Say *normal*. Instead of *norm* say *mort*. (mortal)

# Activity Eleven*****

Warm-up

**Directions: Show the student the following three pictures.**

Ask: Look at the pictures. (shamrock, freckle, jack-o-lantern)
-Which word has the most syllables? (jack-o-lantern-4)
-Reverse the first sound in each syllable in *shamrock*. (ramshock)
-Say *ramshock*. Change the *shock* to *shackle*. (ramshackle)
-Take the first syllable in *shamrock* and the last syllable in *freckle* and make a new word. (shamkle)
-Now take the first syllable in *freckle* and the last syllable in *jack-o-lantern* and make a new word. (frecktern)

Part II

**Phoneme Switch**
Switch the first sounds in the words *jump rope*. (rump jope)
Switch the first sounds in the words *boat dock*. (doat bock)
Switch the first sounds in the words *bone fragment*. (fone bragment)
Switch the first sounds in the words *laser beams*. (baser leams)
Switch the first sounds in the words *kitchen sink*. (sitchen kink)
Switch the first sounds in the words *foam mattress*. (moam fattress)

**Syllable Substitution**
Say *underline*. Instead of *line*, say *shirt*. (undershirt)
Say *turnover*. Instead of *over*, say *pike*. (turnpike)
Say *murder*. Instead of *der,* say *mur*. (murmur)
Say *sunburn*. Instead of *burn* say *burst*. (sunburst)
Say *surplus*. Instead of *plus* say *prize*. (surprise)
Say *turban*. Instead of *ban*, say *tle*. (turtle)
Say *princess*. Instead of *prin*, say *re*. (recess)

# Activity Twelve*****

Warm-up

**Directions: Show the student the following three pictures.**

Ask: Look at the pictures. (teapot, microwave, hexagon)
-How many syllables are in each of these words? (2, 3, 3)
-Take the first syllable in *teapot* and the last syllables in *microwave*. What's the new word? (teawave)
-Now take the first syllable in *hexagon* and the middle syllable in *microwave* and the last syllable in *teapot* and make a new word. (hexcropot)
-Switch the first and last syllables in *hexcropot*. (potcrohex)
-Take the first and last sounds in *microwave* and reverse them. (vicrowame)
-Take the first sound in each syllable of *teapot* and reverse them. (peatot)

Part II

**Phoneme Reversal**
**Say these words backwards.**
| | |
|---|---|
| *mash* | (sham) |
| *slosh* | (shawls) |
| *slate* | (tails) |
| *stile* | (lights) |
| *tine* | (night) |
| *ticks* | (skit) |

**Supply Initial Sound in Words**
What sound do you hear in *thunder* that's missing in *under*? (/th/)
What sound do you hear in *farmer* that's missing in *armor*? (/f/)
What sound do you hear in *blend* that's missing in *lend*? (/b/)
What sound do you hear in *prince* that's missing in *rinse*? (/p/)
What sound do you hear in *slow* that's missing in *low*. (/s/)
What sound do you hear in *grunt* that's missing in *runt*. (/g/)

# Activity Thirteen*****

Warm-up

**Directions: Show the student the following three pictures.**

Ask: Look at the pictures. (kazoo, armadillo, igloo)
-What two words have the same ending sound? (kazoo, igloo)
-How many syllables are in armadillo? (4)
-Take off the second syllable in *armadillo*. (armdillo)
-Take off the last syllable in *armdillo*. (armdill)
-Switch the syllables in *armdill*. (dillarm)
-Take the first syllable in *kazoo*, the third syllable in *armadillo*, and the last syllable in *igloo* to make a word. (kadilloo)
-Take the first and last sounds in *amadillo* and switch them. (ormadilla)

Part II

**Substituting Phonemes in Words (some nonsense)**
Say *meditate*. Instead of the first /t/ say /k/. (medicate)
Say *entirely*. Instead of /l/, say /t/. (entirety)
Say *urchin*. Instead of /ch/ say /b/. (urban)
Say *entrench*. Instead of /t/ say /g/. (engrench)
Say *stabilize*. Instead of /b/, say /m/. (tamilize)
Say *splutter*. Instead of /u/, say /a/. (splatter)

**Phoneme Switcheroo**
Reverse the initial phonemes in the following words:
*weekend meeting*            (meekend weeting)
*second husband*             (hecond susband)
*suit jacket*                (juit sacket)
*full moon*                  (mull foon)

# Activity Fourteen*****

Warm-up

**Directions: Show the student the following three pictures.**

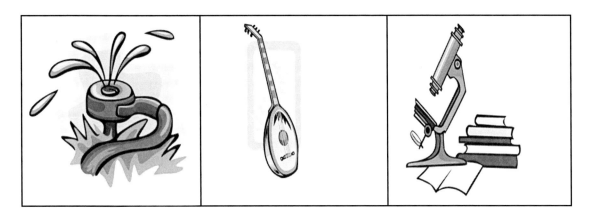

Ask: Look at the pictures. (sprinkler, ukulele, microscope)
-What blend do you hear at the beginning of *sprinkler*? (/spr/)
-How many syllables are in each of these words? (2, 4, 3)
-Take the first and last syllables in *microscope* and switch them. (scopecromi)
-Take the first syllable in *sprinkler* and the last syllable in *microscope* and make a new word. (sprinkscope)
-Say *ukulele* without the third syllable. (ukulee)
-Add /ch/ to the beginning of *ukulee*. (chukulee)
-Add /p/ to the end of *chukulee*. (chukuleep)

Part II

**Substituting Vowel Sounds in Words**
Say *scholarship*. Instead of /ŏ/, say /ē/. (scheelership)
Say *maritime*. Instead of /ī/, say /oi/. (maritoim)
Say *depression*. Instead of /e/ say /u-e/. (deprusion)
Say *bazooka*. Instead of /oo/ say /a/. (bazaka)
Say *suspenseful*. Instead of /e/ say /oo/. (suspoonseful)

**Syllable Manipulation**
Take the second syllable in *confiscate* and put it first. (fisconcate)
Take the second syllable in *translator* and put it first. (latranstor)
Take the second syllable in *cornerstone* and put it first. (ercornstone)
Take the second syllable in *windbreaker* and put it first. (breakwinder)
Take the second syllable in *wastebasket* and put it first. (baswasteket)
Take the second syllable in *grandparent* and put it first. (pargrandent)
Take the second syllable in *thunderstorm* and put it first. (derthundstorm)

# Activity Fifteen*****

Warm-up

**Directions: Show the student the following three pictures.**

Ask: Look at the pictures. (quiet, flamenco dancers, skyscrape)
-How many syllables are in each of these words? (2, 3, 3)
-What blends are in these words? (/fl/, /sk/)
-Say *skyscraper* without the last syllable. (skyscrape)
-Reverse the syllables in *quiet*. (etquī)
-Take the first syllable in *skyscraper*, the second syllable in *flamenco,* and the last syllable in *quiet* and make a new word. (skymenet)
-Say *quiet* without the first sound. (iet)
-Add /r/ to the beginning of *iet*. (riot)

Part II

**Phoneme Reversal**
Say *shack* backwards. (cash)
Say *came* backwards. (make)
Say *speak* backwards. (keeps)
Say *stock* backwards. (cots)
Say *stiff* backwards. (fits)
Say *skill* backward. (licks)

**Sound Deletion**
Say *number* without the /b/. (nummer)
Say *humble* without the /b/. (Hummel)
Say *homely* without the /m/. (holy)
Say *blend* without the /l/. (bend)
Say *swelter* without the /l/. (sweater)
Say *sprout* without the /r/. (spout)
Say *graze* without the /z/. (gray)

# Activity Sixteen*****

Warm-up

**Directions: Show the student the following three pictures.**

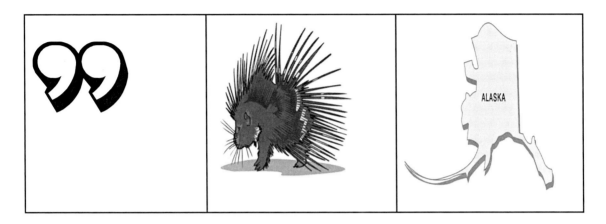

Ask: Look at the pictures. (quotation, porcupine, Alaska)
-Which word has a vowel sound at the beginning of it? (Alaska)
-How many syllables are in each word? (3, 3, 3)
-Which two words have the same ending sound in them? (quotation, porcupine)
-Take the first and the last sounds in *porcupine* and switch them. (norcupipe)
-Say *quotation* without the second syllable. (quotion)
-Say *porcupine* without the second syllable. (porpine)
-Take the first syllable in each of these words to make a new word. (quoporŭ)
-Take the second syllable in each of these words to make a new word. (taycuelas)
-Replace the first sound in *quotation* with /n/. (notation)

Part II

**Phoneme Reversal**
**Take the first sounds in each syllable and switch them.**
| | |
|---|---|
| *complex* | (pomclex) |
| *textbook* | (bexttook) |
| *pretext* | (trepext) |
| *mistake* | (tismake) |
| *dispatch* | (pisdatch) |
| *highway* | (wighhay) |

**Syllable Substitution**
Say *typical*. Instead of *cal*, say *fī*. (typify)
Say *tentacle*. Instead of *cle*, say *tive*. (tentative)
Say *determine*. Instead of *min*, say *ent*. (deterrent)

# Activity Seventeen*****

Warm-up

**Directions: Show the student the following three pictures.**

Ask: Look at the pictures. (necklace, newspaper, Uncle Sam)
-What two words begin with the same sound? (necklace, newspaper-/n/)
-How many syllables are in each word? (2, 3, 3)
-Switch the first and last sounds in *necklace* and make a new word. (secklan)
-Delete the first sound in *newspaper* and make a new word. (ewspapen)
-Take the first syllable in *necklace* and the second syllable in *uncle* and make a new word. (neckle)
-Take the second syllable in *newspaper* and the second syllable in *necklace* to make a new word. (papelace)
-Reverse the words *Uncle Sam*. (Sam Uncle)

Part II

**Sound Isolation**
What sound do you hear in *joint* that's missing in *join*? (/t/)
What sound do you hear in *blooming* that's missing in *booming*? (/l/)
What sound do you hear in *bungee* that's missing in *bunny*? (/j/)
What sound do you hear in *candy* that's missing in *caddy*? (/n/)
What sound do you hear in *pastry* that's missing in *pasty*? (/r/)

**Phoneme Reversal**
**Say these words backwards.**
*late*        (tale)
*dock*        (cod)
*sail*        (lace)
*foal*        (loaf)

# Activity Eighteen*****

Warm-up

**Directions: Show the student the following three pictures.**

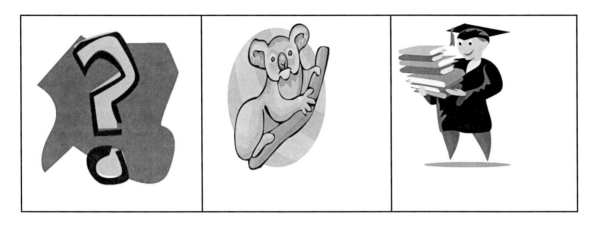

Ask: Look at the pictures. (question mark, koala, graduate)
-What word ends with a vowel sound? (koala)
-How many syllables are there in each word? (4, 3, 3)
-What blend do you hear at the beginning of *graduate*? (/gr/)
-Reverse the first sounds in *question* and *mark* and make a new word. (mestion quark)
-Take the first and last sounds in *graduate* and reverse them. (traduāg)
-Take the first syllable in *question* and the first syllable in *koala* and make a new word. (queskoe)
-Take the last syllable in *question mark,* the last syllable in *koala*, and the first syllable in *graduate* to make a new word. (marklagrad)

Part II

**Pig Latin**
Use Pig Latin to say *welcome*. (elcomeway)
Use Pig Latin to say *blame*. (lamebay)
Use Pig Latin to say *reason*. (easonray)
Use Pig Latin to say *big deal*. (igbay ealday)
Use Pig Latin to say *flirting*. (lirtingfay)
Use Pig Latin to say *honey moon*. (oneyhay oonmay)

**First Sound Switcheroo**
Switch the first sounds in *bobby pins*. (pobby bins)
Switch the first sounds in *blackened fish*. (flackened bish)
Switch the first sounds in *right now*. (night rou)
Switch the first sounds in *hot bath*. (bot-hath)

# Activity Nineteen*****

Warm-up

**Directions: Show the student the following three pictures.**

Ask: Look at the pictures. (field hockey, donkey, campfire)
-What two words have the same number of syllables? (donkey, campfire)
-What two words end with the same sound? (field hockey, donkey-/ē/)
-Reverse the first sounds in each word in *field hockey*. (hield fockey)
-Reverse the first sounds in each syllable in *campfire*. (fampkire)
-Reverse the words *field hockey*. (hockey field)
-Take the first syllable in *field hockey*, the last syllable in *donkey*, and the last syllable in *campfire* to make a new word. (fieldeyfire)
-Say *field hockey* in Pig Latin. (eeldfay ockeyhay)

Part II

**Working With Beginning Blends**
Think of a two syllable word that begins with the blend /sl/.
Think of a two syllable word that begins with the blend /br/.
Think of a two syllable word that begins with the blend /sn/.
Think of a two syllable word that begins with the blend /cl/.
Think of a two syllable word that begins with the blend /tr/.
Think of a two syllable word that begins with the blend /scr/.

**Substituting Sounds in Words**
Say *round*. Instead of /n/, put in a /z/. (roused)
Say *rebel*. Instead of /b/, put in a /v/. (revel)
Say *gopher*. Instead of /f/, put in a /d/. (goader)
Say *scope*. Instead of /k/, put in a /l/. (slope)
Say *paint*. Instead of /n/, put in a /s/. (paste)

# Activity Twenty*****

Warm-up

**Directions: Show the student the following three pictures.**

Ask: Look at the pictures. (asparagus, hippopotamus, jellyfish)
-How many syllables are in each of these words? (4, 5, 3)
-What two words end with the same sound? (asparagus, hippopotamus-/s/)
-Say *jellyfish* without the second syllable. (jellfish)
-Reverse the first and last syllables in *jellyfish*. (fishyjell)
-Say each word in *jelly fish* in Pig Latin. (ellyjay ishfay)
-Take the first sound in each word of *jelly fish* and reverse them. (fellyjish)
-Take the first syllable in *asparagus* and the third syllable in *hippopotamus* and the last syllable in *jellyfish* and make a new word. (upotfish)
-Say *hippopotamus* in Pig Latin. (ippopotamushay)

Part II

**Syllable Deletion (Some Nonsense)**
Say *serviceman* without the second syllable. (serman)
Say *misrepresent* without the second syllable. (misresent)
Say *stumblebum* without the second syllable. (stumbum)
Say *prosperity* without the second syllable. (prosity)
Say *perpendicular* without the second syllable. (pericular)
Say *education* without the third syllable. (edution)

**Substituting Syllables in Words (some nonsense)**
Say *gorgeous*. Instead of *juss*, say *illa*. (gorilla)
Say *moonraker*. Instead of *rake*, say *walk*. (moonwalker)
Say *intimidate*. Instead of *tim*, say *fume*. (infumidate)
Say *straightforward*. Instead of *for*, say *back*. (straightbackward)

# Activity Twenty-One*****

Warm-up

**Directions: Show the student the following three pictures.**

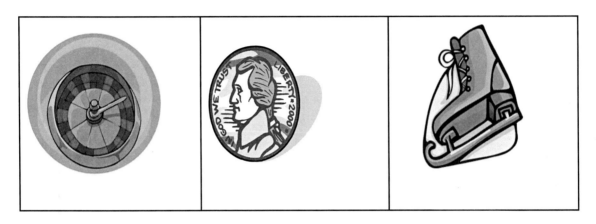

Ask: Look at the pictures. (roulette, nickel, ice-skate)
-How many syllables are in each of these words? (2, 2, 2)
-What blend do you hear at the beginning of *skate*? (/sk/)
-What two words have the same ending sound? (roulette, ice skate-/t/)
-Say *roulette* in Pig Latin. (oulette-ray)
-Reverse the first and last sounds in *nickel* (licken)
-Take the last sound in *ice skate* and put it first. (ticeskay)
-Take the first syllable in *nickel* and the last syllable in *roulette* and make a word. (nickette)
-Take the last syllable in *ice-skate*, the last syllable in *nickel*, and the last syllable in *roulette* and make a new word. (skatelette)

Part II

**Sound Switcheroo**
Reverse the first and last sounds in *suffocate* and make a new word. (tuffocase)
Reverse the first and last sounds in *demote* and make a new word. (temode)
Reverse the first and last sounds in *paralyze* and make a new word. (zaralype)
Reverse the first and last sounds in *grapefruit*. (trapefruig)
Reverse the first and last sounds in *submerge*. (jubmerse)
Reverse the first and last sounds in *plastic*. (clastip)

**Phoneme Substitution**
Say *cypress*. Instead of /p/, say /d/. (cydress)
Say *document*. Instead of /m/, say /b/. (docubent)
Say *fruitfly*. Instead of /t/, say /m/. (fruimfly)
Say *someplace*. Instead of /p/, say /k/. (someclase)

# Activity Twenty-Two*****

Warm-up

**Directions: Show the student the following three pictures.**

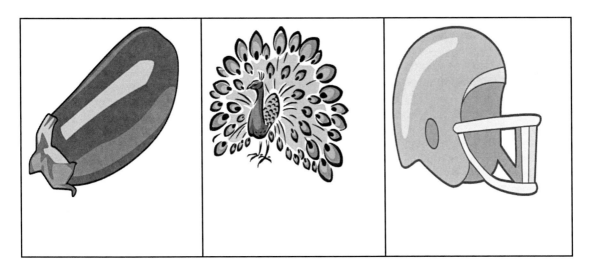

Ask: Look at the pictures. (eggplant, peacock, helmet)
-How many syllables are in each word? (2, 2, 2)
-What words end with the same sound? (eggplant, helmet-/t/)
-Reverse the first and last sounds in *peacock*. (keacop)
-Reverse the first and last sounds in *helmet*. (met-hel)
-Say *peacock* in Pig Latin. (eacockpay)
-Say *helmet* in Pig Latin. (elmethay)
-Take the first syllable in *eggplant* and the last syllable in *helmet* and make a new word. (eggmet)
-Take the first syllable in *peacock* and the last syllable in *eggplant* and make a new word. (peaplant)

Part II

**Syllable Reversal**
Switch the syllables in *sideswipe*. (swipeside)
Switch the syllables in *clamor*. (orclam)
Switch the syllables in *kismet*. (metkis)
Switch the syllables in *manmade*. (mademan)
Switch the syllables in *knapsack*. (sackknap)

**Vowel Change**
Change the second vowel sound in *romantic* to /oo/. (romoontic)
Change the third vowel sound in *navigate* to /oi/. (navigoit)
Change the second vowel sound in *surplus* to /ā/. (surplase)

# Activity Twenty-Three*****

Warm-up

**Directions: Show the student the following three pictures.**

Ask: Look at the pictures. (dolphin, unicorn, seahorse)
-What two words end with the same sound? (dolphin, unicorn-/n/)
-Which word has the most syllables? (unicorn-3)
-Which word begins with a long vowel sound? (unicorn-/u-e/)
-Reverse the first and last sounds in *dolphin*. (nolphid)
-Reverse the first sound in each syllable of *seahorse*. (heasorse)
-Say *dolphin* in Pig Latin. (olphinday)
-Say *seahorse* in Pig Latin. (eahorsesay)
-Take the first syllable in *seahorse* and the last syllable in *dolphin* and make a new word. (seaphin)
-Take the first syllable in *dolphin,* the second syllable in *unicorn,* and the last syllable in *seahorse* to make a new word. (dolihorse)

Part II

**Phoneme Switcheroo**
Reverse the first sounds in *road coverage*. (coad roverage)
Reverse the first sounds in *final round*. (rinal found)
Reverse the first sounds in *major championship*. (chajor mampionship)
Reverse the first sounds in *mow lawn*. (low mawn)
Reverse the first sounds in *second place*. (pecond slace)
Reverse the first sounds in *sun devil*. (dun sevil)

**Phoneme Reversal**
Say *lobe* backwards. (bowl)
Say *cope* backwards. (poke)
Say *came* backwards. (make)

# Activity Twenty-Four*****

Warm-up

**Directions: Show the student the following three pictures.**

Ask: Look at the pictures. (computer, snowmobile, pineapple)
-What word has a blend in it? (snowmobile-/sn/)
-What words have the same ending sound? (snowmobile, pineapple-/l/)
-How many syllables are there in each word? (3, 3, 3)
-Say *computer* without the second syllable. (comter)
-Say *snow mobile* without the second syllable. (snowbeel)
-Take the first and last syllables in *computer* and reverse them. (erpūtcom)
-Take the first syllable in *computer*, the second syllable in *snowmobile* and the last syllable in *pineapple* and make a new word. (commople)
-Take the first syllable in *pineapple* and the last syllable in *snowmobile* and make a new word. (pinebeel)
-Take the last syllable in *computer* and put it first. (tercompute)

Part II

**Pig Latin**
Use Pig Latin to say *betray*. (etraybay)
Use Pig Latin to say *favor*. (avorfay)
Use Pig Latin to say *library*. (ibrarylay)
Use Pig Latin to say *grocery bag*. (rocerygay agbay)
Use Pig Latin to say *picture*. (icturepay)
Use Pig Latin to say *blossom*. (lossombay)

**Phoneme Substitution (some nonsense)**
Say *rebuild*. Instead of /b/, say /z/. (rezild)
Say *portray*. Instead of /t/, say /b/. (porbray)
Say *object*. Instead of /j/, say /l/. (oblect)
Say *vocalize*. Instead of /k/, say /m/. (vomalize)

# Activity Twenty-Five*****

Warm-up

**Directions: Show the student the following three pictures.**

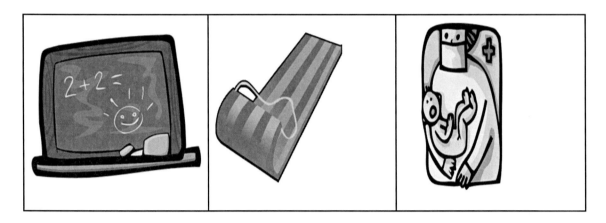

Ask: Look at the pictures. (blackboard, toboggan, obstetrician)
-What blend do you hear at the beginning of *blackboard*? (/bl/)
-How many syllables are in each of these words? (2, 3, 4)
-Say *blackboard* backwards. (boardblack)
-Say *toboggan* without the first syllable. (boggan)
-Say *obstetrician* without the second syllable. (obtrician)
-Reverse the first and last sounds in toboggan. (noboggat)
-Change the first vowel sound in *blackboard* to /ē/. (bleekboard)
-Change the second vowel sound in *toboggan* to /i/. (tobiggan)
-Take the first syllable in *blackboard* and the second syllable in *toboggan* and make a new word. (blackbog)
-Take the first syllable in *obstetrician* and the last syllable in *toboggan* and make a new word. (obgan)

Part II

**Word Generation**
Think of a two syllable word that ends with /sh/.
Think of a two syllable word that ends with /g/.
Think of a two syllable word that ends with /k/.
Think of a two syllable word that ends with /d/.
Think of a two syllable word that ends with /t/.

**Phoneme Reversal**
Reverse the first sounds in *paved way*. (waved pay)
Reverse the first sounds in *baked potato*. (paked botato)
Reverse the first sounds in *gentle Ben*. (bentle jen)
Reverse the first sounds in *come home*. (hum kome)

# Activity Twenty-Six*****

Warm-up

**Directions: Show the student the following three pictures.**

Ask: Look at the pictures. (umbrella, jester, sharpener)
-What two words have the same ending sound? (jester, sharpener-/er/)
-What digraph do you hear at the beginning of *sharpener*? (/sh/)
-How many syllables are in each word? (3, 2, 3)
-Say *sharpener* without the second syllable. (sharper)
-Say *umbrella* without the first syllable. (brella)
-Take the second syllable in *sharpener* and the first syllable in *jester* and make a new word. (enjest)
-Take the second syllable in *umbrella*, the second syllable in *jester,* and the second syllable in *sharpener* to make a new word. (brellterpen)

Part II

**Phoneme Substitution**
Say *slushy*. Instead of /sh/, say /m/. (slummy)
Say *foodstuff*. Instead of /d/, say /l/. (foolstuff)
Say *childish*. Instead of /ī/, say /oi/. (choildish)
Say *deform*. Instead of /f/, say /n/. (denorm)
Say *combat*. Instead of /m/, say /l/. (colbat)

**Syllable Deletion**
Say *excitable* without the second syllable. (extable)
Say *magnetic* without the second syllable. (mag-ic)
Say *refinement* without the last syllable. (refine)
Say *mesmerize* without the second syllable. (mezize)
Say *sunflower* without the second syllable. (suner)
Say *confinement* without the second syllable. (conment)

# Activity Twenty-Seven*****

Warm-up

**Directions: Show the student the following three pictures.**

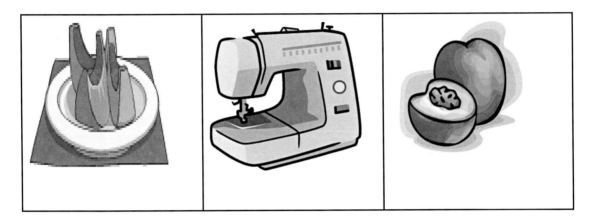

Ask: Look at the pictures. (cantaloupe, sewing machine, nectarine)
-What two words have the same ending sound? (sewing machine, nectarine)
-How many syllables are in each of these words? (3, 4, 3)
-Reverse the first sounds in each word in *sewing machine*. (mowing sachine)
-Take the first and last sounds in *cantaloupe* and reverse them. (pantaloke)
-Say *nectarine* without the first syllable. (tarine)
-Take the first syllable in *cantaloupe* and the last syllable in *sewing machine* and make a new word. (cansheen)
-Take the first syllable in *nectarine* and the first syllable in *sewing machine* and make a new word. (necksew)

Part II

**Syllable Reversal**
Reverse the syllables in *muster*. (termus)
Reverse the syllables in *neglect*. (glectne)
Reverse the syllables in *ransack*. (sackran)
Reverse the syllables in *turnstile*. (stileturn)
Reverse the syllables in *transfer*. (fertrans)
Reverse the syllables in *courtyard*. (yardcourt)

**Phoneme Switcheroo**
Reverse the first sounds in each syllable of *sourpuss*. (powerrsuss)
Reverse the first sounds in each syllable of *mudhole*. (hudmole)
Reverse the first sounds in each syllable of *mushroom*. (rushmoom)
Reverse the first sounds in each syllable of *robust*. (borust)
Reverse the first sounds in each syllable of vacate. (kavate)
Reverse the first sounds in each syllable of distend. (tisdend)

# Activity Twenty-Eight*****

Warm-up

**Directions: Show the student the following three pictures.**

Ask: Look at the pictures. (gypsy, dictionary, skeleton)
-What two words have the same ending sound? (gypsy, dictionary)
-What blend do you hear at the beginning of *skeleton*? (/sk/)
-How many syllables are in each word? (2, 4, 3)
-Say *skeleton* without the second syllable. (skelton)
-Say *dictionary* without the first syllable. (tionary)
-Take the first syllable in *gypsy* and the second syllable in *dictionary* and make a new word. (gyption)
-Take the first syllable in *skeleton*, and the last syllable in *gypsy* and make a new word. (skelsy)
-Say *dictionary*. Instead of /k/ say /p/. (diptionary)
-Take the first syllable in *gypsy*, the third syllable in *dictionary*, and the last syllable in *skeleton* and make a new word. (gyparton)

Part II

**Pig Latin**
Say *minor cut* in Pig Latin. (inormay utcay)
Say *cheese pizza* in Pig Latin. (eese-chay izza-pay)
Say *blue tooth* in Pig Latin. (loobay oothtay)
Say *chemical test* in Pig Latin. (emicalkay esttay)

**Vowel Substitution**
Change the vowel sound in *cream* to /ĕ/. (crem)
Change the vowel sound in *scream* to /ŭ/. (scrum)
Change the vowel sound in *grain* to /ĭ/. (grin)
Change the vowel sound in *blast* to /ĕ/. (blest)

# Activity Twenty-Nine*****

Warm-up

**Directions: Show the student the following three pictures.**

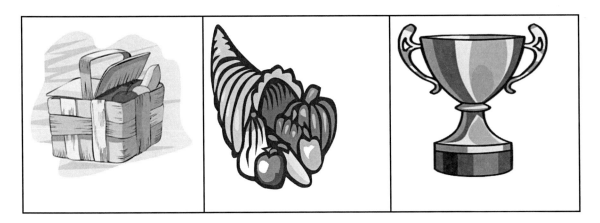

Ask: Look at the pictures. (basket, cornucopia, trophy)
-What word has a blend in it? (trophy-/tr/)
-How many syllables are in each word? (2, 5, 2)
-Reverse the first and last sounds in *basket*. (taskeb)
-Switch the first and last sounds in *trophy*. (ee-ropht)
-Take off the second syllable in *cornucopia*. (corncopia)
-Reverse the syllables in *basket*. (ketbask)
-Take the first syllable in *basket* and the last syllable in *trophy* and make a new word. (basphy)
-Take the first syllable in *cornucopia* and the second syllable in *basket* and make a new word. (cornket)

Part II

**Phoneme Isolation (Some Nonsense)**
What sound do you hear in *respect* that's missing in *resect*? (/p/)
What sound do you hear in *retired* that's missing in *retied*? (/r/)
What sound do you hear in *retrain* that's missing in *retain*? (/r/)
What sound do you hear in *trifle* that's missing in *trial*? (/f/)
What sound do you hear in *godless* that's missing in *goddess*? (/l/)

**Phoneme Switcheroo**
Reverse the first sounds in *brought tears*. (trought beers)
Reverse the first sounds in *black Friday*. (flack briday)
Reverse the first sounds in *red barn*. (bed rarn)
Reverse the first sounds in *television show*. (shelevision tow)
Reverse the first sounds in *missing goblet*. (gissing moblet)

# Activity Thirty*****

Warm-up

**Directions: Show the student the following three pictures.**

Ask: Look at the pictures. (archery, spaghetti, briefcase)
-What two words have the same ending sound? (archery, spaghetti-/ē/)
-How many syllables are in each word? (4, 3, 3)
-What blends do you hear in these words? (/sp/, /br/)
-Say *archery* without the second syllable. (archy)
-Reverse the syllables in *briefcase*. (casebrief)
-Reverse the first sounds in each syllable of *briefcase*. (criefbase)
-Switch the first and last sounds in *briefcase*. (sriefcabe)
-Take the first syllable in *archery* and the last syllable in *briefcase* and make a new word. (archcase)
-Take the second syllable in *spaghetti,* the second syllable in *archery,* and the last syllable in *briefcase* to make a word. (getercase)

Part II

**Pig Latin**
Say *migrate* in Pig Latin. (igratemay)
Say *blossom* in Pig Latin. (lossombay)
Say *picnic* in Pig Latin. (icnicpay)
Say *traitor* in Pig Latin. (raitortay)
Say *movie star* in Pig Latin. (ooviemay tarsay)
Say *flower* in Pig Latin. (lour-fay)

**Final Consonant Isolation**
Think of a word that doesn't rhyme with but has the same last sound as *slosh.*
Think of a word that doesn't rhyme with but has the same last sound as *judgment.*
Think of a word that doesn't rhyme with but has the same last sound as *watch.*

# Activity Thirty-One*****

Warm-up

**Directions: Show the student the following three pictures.**

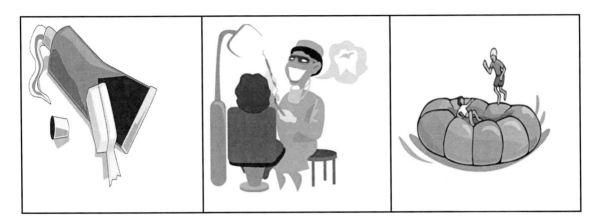

Ask: Look at the pictures. (toothpaste, dentist, trampoline)
-What two words have the same ending sound? (toothpaste, dentist)
-How many syllables are in each word? (2, 2, 3)
-What word has a blend in it? (trampoline-/tr/)
-Reverse the syllables in *dentist*. (tistden)
-Reverse the syllables in *toothpaste*. (paste tooth)
-Switch first sound in each syllable in *toothpaste*. (poothtaste)
-Switch the first sound in each syllable in *dentist* . (tendist)
-Take the first syllable in *toothpaste* and the second syllable in *dentist* to make a new word. (toothtist)
-Take the first syllable in *dentist* and the last syllable in *trampoline* and make a new word. (denlean)

Part II

**Phoneme Substitution (Some Nonsense)**
Say *inferior*. Instead of /f/, say /t/. (interior)
Say *infest*. Instead of /f/, say /j/. (injest)
Say *traitor*. Instead of /t/, say /n/. (trainer)
Say *thrifty*. Instead of /f/, say /s/. (thristy)
Say *standoff*. Instead of /d/, say /p/. (stanpoff)

**Sound Isolation**
What sound do you hear in *runaway* that's missing in *runway*? (/u/)
What sound do you hear in *skimpy* that's missing in *skippy*? (/m/)
What sound do you hear in *shrewd* that's missing in *shooed*? (/r/)
What sound do you hear in *nasty* that's missing in *natty*? (/s/)

# Activity Thirty-Two*****

Warm-up

**Directions: Show the student the following three pictures.**

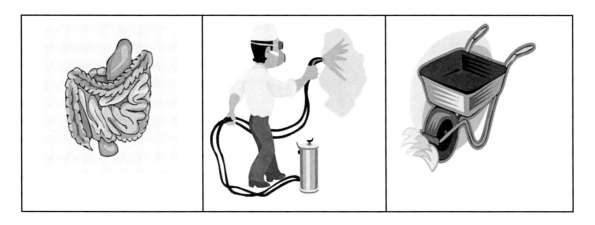

Ask: Look at the pictures. (intestine, insulation, wheelbarrow)
-What two words have the same ending sound? (intestine, insulation)
-How many syllables are in each word? (3, 4, 3)
-Reverse the syllables in *wheelbarrow*. (barrowwheel)
-Take off the last syllable in *wheelbarrow*. (wheelbare)
-Take off the last syllable in *intestine*. (intes)
-Take off the first syllable in *insulation*. (sulation)
-Reverse the first sounds in each syllable in *wheelbarrow*. (beelwharrow)
-Take the second syllable in *intestine* and the last syllable in *insulation* and make a new word. (testion)
-Take the second syllable in *intestine,* the second syllable in *insulation*, and the last syllable in *wheelbarrow* and make a new word. (tessulow)

Part II

**Phoneme Switcheroo**
Switch the first sound in each word .
*hot dog* (dot hog)
*text book* (bext took)
*paper towel* (taper powel)
*pumpernickel bread* (bumpernickel pread)

**Syllable Deletion**
Say *temporary* without the second syllable. (temary)
Say *fascinate* without the second syllable. (fasate)
Say *Atlantic* without the second syllable. (attic)
Say *hobgoblin* without the second syllable. (hoblin)
Say *transference* without the second syllable. (transence)

# Activity Thirty-Three*****

Warm-up

**Directions: Show the student the following three pictures.**

Ask: Look at the pictures. (Liberty Bell, marionette, popsicle)
-What two words have the same ending sound? (Liberty Bell, popsicle-/l/)
-How many syllables are in each word? (4, 4, 3)
-Say popsicle in Pig Latin. (opsicle-pay)
-Take the first sound in each word in *Liberty Bell* and reverse them. (biberty lell)
-Take the first sound in each syllable in maypole and reverse them. (paymole)
-Take the first and last sounds in *marionette* and reverse them. (tarionem)
-Take the last syllable in *Liberty Bell* and the last syllable in *marionette* and make a new word. (bellnette)
-Take the second syllable in *maypole* and the last syllable in *marionette* and make a new word. (polette)

Part II

**Syllable Addition**
Add *roo* to the beginning of *teen*. (routine)
Add *rum* to the beginning of *pus*. (rumpus)
Add *mis* to the beginning of *tress*. (mistress)
Add *scrim* to the beginning of *ej*. (scrimmage)
Add *out* to the beginning of *live*. (outlive)
Add *ob* to the beginning of *skure*. (obscure)

**Phoneme Switch**
Reverse the first and last sounds in *thief*. (feeth)
Reverse the first and last sounds in *sideburn*. (nideburs)
Reverse the first and last sounds in *material*. (lateriam)
Reverse the first and last sounds in *justice*. (sustij)

# Activity Thirty-Four*****

Warm-up

**Directions: Show the student the following three pictures.**

Ask: Look at the pictures. (dynamite, candy cane, blanket)
-What two words have the same ending sound? (dynamite, blanket)
-What word has a blend in it? (blanket-/bl/)
-How many syllables are in each word? (3, 3, 2)
-Take the first sound in *candy* and the last sound in *cane* and reverse them. (nandy cake)
-Take the first and last sounds in *dynamite* and reverse them. (tynomide)
-Take the first and last syllables in *dynamite* and reverse them. (mite-a-dyne)
-Take the first syllable in *blanket*, the second syllable in *dynamite* and the second syllable in *candy cane* and make a new word. (blankudee)
-Say *blanket* in Pig Latin. (lanketbay)

Part II

**Pig Latin**
Say *black corvette* in Pig Latin. (lackbay orvettekay)
Say *jumper cable* in Pig Latin. (umperjay ablekay)
Say *planter* in Pig Latin. (lanterpay)
Say *fuzzy bear* in Pig Latin. (buzzy fare)
Say *notebook* in Pig Latin. (ote-booknay)
Say *transport* in Pig Latin. (ransporttay)

**Syllable Substitution**
Say *dispose*. Instead of *pose* say *pense*. (dispense)
Say *sidestep*. Instead of *step* say *swipe*. (sideswipe)
Say *distracted*. Instead of *tract* say *trust*. (distrusted)
Say *delighted*. Instead of *lighted* say *number*. (denumber)

# Activity Thirty-Five*****

Warm-up

**Directions: Show the student the following three pictures.**

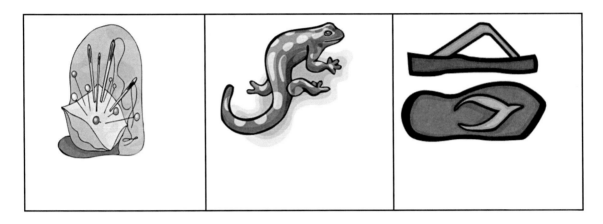

Ask: Look at the pictures. (pincushion, salamander, flip-flop)
-What words have the same first vowel sound in them? (pincushion, flip-flop-/ĭ/)
-What word has a digraph in it? (pincushion-/sh/)
-How many syllables are in each of these words? (3, 4, 2)
-Reverse the first and last sounds in *pincushion* and make a new word
  (nincushup)
-Delete the last syllable in *salamander*. (salamand)
-Reverse the first and last sounds in *flip-flop*. (plip flof)
-Say *salamander* without the second syllable. (salmander)
-Take the first syllable in *pincushion,* the second syllable in *salamander,* and the last
  syllable in *flip-flop* and make a new word. (pinaflop)
-Take the third syllable in *salamander* and the first syllable in *pincushion* and make a
  new word. (manpin)

Part II

**Phoneme Switch**
Switch the first and last sounds in *turner* and make a new word. (rurnet)
Switch the first and last sounds in *muffin* and make a new word. (nuffim)
Switch the first and last sounds in *peanut* and make a new word. (teanup)
Switch the first and last sounds in *pirate* and make a new word. (tirape)
Switch the first and last sounds in *return* and make a new word. (netur)

**Vowel Substitution**
Say *master*. Instead of /ă/, say /u/. (muster)
Say *grind*. Instead of /ī/, say /ou/. (ground)
Say *soft*. Instead of /ŏ/ say /ĭ/. (sift)
Say *flint*. Instead of /ĭ/, say /aw/. (flaunt)

# Activity Thirty-Six*****

Warm-up

**Directions: Show the student the following three pictures.**

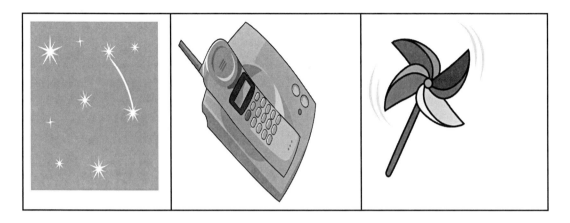

Ask: Look at the pictures. (constellation, telephone, pinwheel)
-What two words have the same ending sound? (constellation, telephone)
-How many syllables are in each word? (4, 3, 2)
-Reverse the first and last sounds in *constellation* and make a new word. (nonstellashuck)
-Reverse the first and last sounds in *telephone*. (nelephote)
-Reverse the first and last sounds in *pinwheel*. (linwheep)
-Say *constellation* without the third syllable. (constelltion)
-Reverse the syllables in *pinwheel*. (wheelpin)
-Now switch the first sound in each syllable of *pinwheel*. (winpeel)
-Take the first syllable in *constellation,* the second syllable in *telephone*, and the first syllable in *pinwheel* to make a new word. (conuppin)
-Take the last syllable in *pinwheel* and the last syllable in *telephone* and make a new word. (wheelphone)

Part II

**Syllable Reversal**
Reverse the first and last syllables in *passerby*. (byerpass)
Reverse the first and last syllables in *spectator*. (ertaspec)
Reverse the first and last syllables in *sunflower*. (erflowsun)
Reverse the first and last syllables in *firepower*. (erpowfire)
Reverse the first and last syllables in *fantastic*. (tictasfan)

**Pig Latin**
Say *shave* in Pig Latin. (ave-shay)
Say *control* in Pig Latin. (ontrolkay)
Say *hair-do* in Pig Latin. (air-do-hay)

143

# Activity Thirty-Seven*****

Warm-up

**Directions: Show the student the following three pictures.**

Ask: Look at the pictures. (hot air balloon, nail polish, flashlight)
-What two words have the same digraph in them? (polish, flashlight-/sh/)
-How many syllables are in each word? (4, 3, 2)
-Reverse the syllables in *flash light.* (lightflash)
-Reverse the first and last sounds in *nail polish* and make a new word. (shail polin)
-Say *nail polish* without the second syllable. (nailish)
-Say *flashlight* in Pig Latin. (lashlightfay)
-Take the first syllable in *hot air balloon,* the first syllable in *nail polish*, and the last syllable in *flashlight* and make a word. (hotnaillight)
-Take the second syllable in *hot air balloon*, the second syllable in *nail polish,* and the first syllable in *flashlight* to make a new word. (airpolflash)

Part II

**Syllable Deletion**
Take off the second syllable in *magnificent.* (mag-i-cent)
Take off the second syllable in *postmaster.* (poster)
Take off the second syllable in *selfdestruct.* (selfstruct)
Take off the second syllable in *shipbuilder.* (shipper)
Take off the second syllable in *typical.* (typcal)

**Phoneme Switcheroo**
Reverse the first and last sounds in *forecast.* (torecasf)
Reverse the first and last sounds in *bailiff.* (failib)
Reverse the first and last sounds in *because.* (zecaub)
Reverse the first and last sounds in *much.* (chum)
Reverse the first and last sounds in *label.* (label)
Reverse the first and last sounds in *change.* (jānch)

# Activity Thirty-Eight*****

Warm-up

**Directions: Show the student the following three pictures.**

Ask: Look at the pictures. (shower head, light bulb, snowball fight)
-What word has a digraph in it? (showerhead-/sh/)
-How many syllables are in each word? (3, 2, 3)
-Reverse the first and last sounds in *shower head*. (dowerhesh)
-Reverse the first and last sounds in *lightbulb*. (bightbull)
-Reverse the words in *snowball fight*. (fight snowball)
-Say *snowball fight* without the second syllable. (snowfight)
-Reverse the first sound in each word in *light bulb*. (bightlulb)
-Take the first syllable in *light bulb* and the second syllable in *shower head* and make a new word. (lighter)
-Take the third syllable in *showerhead* and the last syllable in *snowball fight* and make a new word. (headfight)

Part II

**Phoneme Deletion**
Say *pointless* without the /l/. (pointess)
Say *mystic* without the /t/. (mysic)
Say *embroil* without the /r/. (emboil)
Say *sander* without the /n/. (sadder)

**Pig Latin**
Say *stampede* in Pig Latin. (tampedesay)
Say *plane trip* in Pig Latin. (lanepay riptay)
Say *beautiful* in Pig Latin. (utifulbay)
Say *dandy* in Pig Latin. (andyday)
Say *pupil* in Pig Latin. (upilpay)

# Activity Thirty-Nine*****

Warm-up

**Directions: Show the student the following three pictures.**

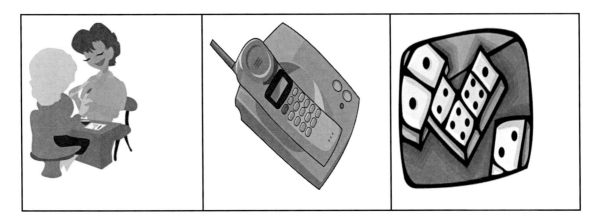

Ask: Look at the pictures. (manicure, telephone, dominoes)
-How many syllables are in each word? (3, 3, 3)
-Reverse the first and last sounds in *manicure* and make a new word. (ranicume)
-Reverse the first and last sounds in *telephone* to make a new word. (nelephont)
-Take the last syllable in *domino* and put it first to make a new word. (o-dom-in)
-Say *dominos* without the second syllable. (domnoes)
-Say *manicure* without the second syllable. (mancure)
-Reverse the first and last syllables in *telephone*. (phon-e-tell)
-Take the first syllable in *manicure,* the second syllable in *telephone*, and the last syllable in *dominoes* to make a new word. (manenoes)
-Take the first syllable in *dominoes*, the second syllable in *manicure,* and the last syllable in *telephone* to make a word. (domiphone)

Part II

**Syllable Substitution**
Say *plankton*. Instead of *ton*, say *yard*. (plankyard)
Say *pendant*. Instead of *dant,* say *guin*. (penguin)
Say *self-control.* Instead of *troll,* say *fess*. (self-confess)
Say *projector.* Instead of *tor,* say *tile*. (projectile)
Say *pedicure.* Instead of *cure,* say *gree*. (pedigree)

**Syllable Deletion**
Say *perspective* without the second syllable. (pertive)
Say *manhandle* without the second syllable. (mandle)
Say *granular* without the second syllable. (granlar)
Say *furnishings* without the second syllable. (furnings)

# Activity Forty*****

Warm-up

**Directions: Show the student the following three pictures.**

Ask: Look at the pictures. (extinguisher, candlelight, record player)
-What two words have the same ending sound? (extinguisher, record player-/r/)
-How many syllables are in each word? (4,3, 4)
-What word has a digraph in it? (extinguisher)
-Take off the second syllable in *candlelight*. (canlight)
-Reverse the first and last sounds in *candlelight*. (tandlelike)
-Take off the first syllable in *extinguisher*. (tinguisher)
-Take the first syllable in *extinguisher*, the third syllable in *candlelight,* and the last syllable in *record player* and make a new word. (exlighter)
-Take the third syllable in *record player* and the second syllable in *candlelight* to make a new word. (playdle)

Part II

**Pig Latin**
Say *breakfast* in Pig Latin. (reakfastbay)
Say *truffle* in Pig Latin. (ruffletay)
Say *match point* in Pig Latin. (atchmay ointpay)
Say *tinsel* in Pig Latin. (inseltay)
Say *bagel* in Pig Latin. (agelbay)
Say *decision* in Pig Latin. (ecisionday)

**Phoneme Switcheroo**
Reverse the first sounds in *hard working*. (ward horking)
Reverse the first and last sounds in *large continent*. (karge lontinent)
Reverse the first sounds in *cold pizza*. (pold kizza)
Reverse the first sounds in *costly goof*. (gostly koof)

# Activity Forty-One*****

Warm-up

**Directions: Show the student the following three pictures.**

Ask: Look at the pictures. (mechanic, grandmother, caterpillar)
-What two words have the same ending sound? (caterpillar, grandmother-/r/)
-What word has a blend in it? (grandmother-/gr/)
-How many syllables are in each word? (3, 3 4)
-Reverse the first and last sounds in *mechanic*. (kech-an-im)
-Reverse the first and last sounds in *caterpillar*. (raterpillak)
-Reverse the first and last sounds in *grandmother*. (randmotheg)
-Take the first syllable in *grandmother* and the second syllable in *caterpillar* and make a new word. (grander)
-Take the third syllable in *caterpillar* and the last syllable in *mechanic* to make a new word. (pillic)

Part II
**Syllable Reversal**
Reverse the first and last syllables in *turbojet*. (jetbotur)
Reverse the first and last syllables in *turpentine*. (tinepentur)
Reverse the first and last syllables in *honkytonk*. (tonkyhonk)
Reverse the first and last syllables in *shipbuilder*. (erbuildship)
Reverse the first and last syllables in *fosterchild*. (childerfost)
Reverse the first and last syllables in *capital*. (talicap)

**Vowel Substitution**
Say *turnout*. Instead of /ou/, say /ĭ/. (turnit)
Say *plaster*. Instead of /ă,/ say /oo/. (plooster)
Say *inflect*. Instead of /ĕ/, say /ĭ/. (inflict)
Say *dragon*. Instead of /ă/, say /ŏ/. (drogon)
Say *painful*. Instead of /ā/, say /ĕ/. (penful)

# Activity Forty-Two*****

Warm-up

**Directions: Show the student the following three pictures.**

Ask: Look at the pictures. (trampoline, referee, fire engine)
-What two words have the same ending sound? (trampoline, fire engine-/n/)
-How many syllables are in each word? (3, 3, 3)
-What word has a blend in it? (trampoline-/tr/)
-Reverse the first and last sounds in *fire engine*. (nire enjif)
-Say *trampoline* in Pig Latin. (rampolinetay)
-Reverse the two words in fire engine. (engine fire)
-Say *referee* without the second syllable. (refee)
-Take the first syllable in *referee*, and the last syllable in *fire engine* to make a new word. (refjin)
-Reverse the first and last syllables in *trampoline*.  (lean-po-tram)

Part II
**Sound Isolation**
What sound do you hear in *prize* that's missing in *pry*? (/z/)
What sound do you hear in *shrine* that's missing in *shine*? (/r/)
What sound do you hear in *spore* that's missing in *sore*? (/p/)
What sound do you hear in *child* that's missing in *chide*? (/l/)
What sound do you hear in *smoke* that's missing in *soak*? (/m/)
What sound do you hear in *slide* that's missing in *side*. (/l/)

**Syllable Addition**
Add *ski* to the end of *water*. (waterski)
Add *stake* to the end of *sweep*. (sweepstake)
Add *pile* to the end of *stock*. (stockpile)
Add *dum* to the end of *sel*. (seldom)

# Activity Forty-Three*****

Warm-up

**Directions: Show the student the following three pictures.**

Ask: Look at the pictures. (telescope, parachute, sailboat)
-What two words have the same ending sound? (parachute, sailboat)
-How many syllables are in each word? (3, 3, 2)
-Reverse the syllables in *sailboat.* (boatsail)
-Reverse the first and last syllables in *parachute.* (shootapar)
-Reverse the first and last syllables in *telescope.* (scope-a-tel)
-Take the first syllable in *telescope,* the second syllable in *parachute,* and the last syllable in *sailboat* to make a new word. (telaboat)
-Take the first syllable in *parachute,* and the third syllable in *telescope* to make a new word. (parscope)
-Use Pig Latin to say *sailboat.* (ailboatsay)
-Say *telescope* without the first sound. (elescope)

Part II

**Syllable Substitution (Nonsense Words)**
Say *explanation.* Instead of *tion,* say *ful.* (explanaful)
Say *wonderful.* Instead of *der,* say *ker.* (wonkerful)
Say *dangerous.* Instead of *dan,* say *tie.* (tijerous)
Say *convertible.* Instead of *vert*, say *sit.* (consitible)
Say *information.* Instead of *ma,* say *pu.* (inforpution)

**Vowel Discrimination**
Think of a word that has the same vowel sound as *spawn.*
Think of a word that has the same vowel sound as *blame.*
Think of a word that has the same vowel sound as *street.*
Think of a word that has the same vowel sound as *pluck.*
Think of a word that has the same vowel sound as *boil.*

# Activity Forty-Four*****

Warm-up

**Directions: Show the student the following three pictures.**

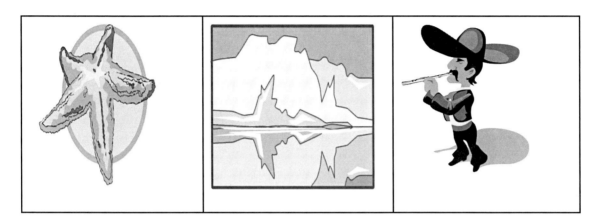

Ask: Look at the pictures. (starfish, iceberg, sombrero)
-What word begins with a blend? (starfish-/st/)
-How many syllables are in each word? (2, 2, 3)
-Reverse the syllables in *starfish*. (fishstar)
-Reverse the syllables in *iceberg*. (berg ice)
-Say *starfish* in Pig Latin. (tarfishsay)
-Say *sombrero* in Pig Latin. (ombrerosay)
-Take the first syllable in *starfish* and the second syllable in *iceberg* and make a new word. (starberg)
-Take the first syllable in *sombrero,* the first syllable in *iceberg*, and the last syllable in *starfish,* and make a new word. (somicefish)

Part II

**Phoneme Switcheroo**
Switch the first and last sounds in *disjoint*. (tisjoind)
Switch the first and last sounds in *thread*. (dreath)
Switch the first and last sounds in *moccasin*. (noccasim)
Switch the first and last sounds in *devote*. (tevode)
Switch the first and last sounds in *dimness*. (simned)
Switch the first and last sounds in *gladness*. (sladneg)

**Initial Phoneme Reversal**
Reverse the first sounds in *lunch date* to make a new word. (dunch late)
Reverse the first sounds in *family meal* to make a new word. (mamily feal)
Reverse the first sounds in *people's vote* to make a new word. (veople's pote)
Reverse the first sounds in *hungry man* to make a new word. (mungry han)

# Activity Forty-Five*****

Warm-up

**Directions: Show the student the following three pictures.**

Ask: Look at the pictures. (pyramid, astronaut, golf cart)
-What two words have the same ending (3, 3, 2)
-Reverse the syllables in *golf cart*. (cart golf)
-Reverse the first sounds in *golf cart*. (colf gart)
-Reverse the first and last syllables in *pyramid*. (midapyr)
-Delete the second syllable in *astronaut*. (asnaut)
-Take the first syllable in *astronaut* and the last syllable in *pyramid* and make a new word. (asmid)
-Say *golf cart* in Pig Latin. (olfgay artkay)
-Say *astronaut* without the first syllable. (tronaut)

Part II

**Syllable Substitution**
Say *birdbath*. Instead of *bath*, say *cage*. (birdcage)
Say *sundown*. Instead of *down*, say *flower*. (sunflower)
Say *outlay*. Instead of lay, say *last*. (outlast)
Say *flashback*. Instead of back, say *bulb*. (flashbulb)
Say *infection*. Instead of *fec*, say *duc*. (induction)

**Sound Isolation**
What sound do you hear in *tread* that's missing in *Ted*? (/r/)
What sound do you hear in *sleepy* that's missing in *seepy*? (/l/)
What sound do you hear in *pleasant* that missing in *peasant*? (/l/)
What sound do you hear in *dread* that's missing in *dead*? (/r/)
What sound do you hear in *break* that's missing in *bake*? (/r/)

# Activity Forty-Six*****

Warm-up

**Directions: Show the student the following three pictures.**

Ask: Look at the pictures. (French fries, ski vest, artist)
-What two words have the same ending sound? (ski vest, artist)
-How many syllables are in each word? (2, 2, 2)
-What two words have a blend at the end? (vest, artist-/st/)
-Reverse the words in *french fries*. (fries french)
-Reverse the words in *ski vest*. (vest ski)
-Use Pig Latin to say *french fries*. (renchfay riesfay)
-Use Pig Latin to say *ski vest*. (keesay estvay)
-Take the first syllable in *artist* and the last syllable in *ski vest* and make a new word. (arvest)
-Add /h/ to the beginning of *arvest*. (harvest)
-Take /r/ out of *French* and *fries* and make a new word. (fench fies)

## Part II

**Sound Isolation**
What sound do you hear in *fable* that's missing in *fail*? (/b/)
What sound do you hear in *splashed* that's missing in *slashed*? (/p/)
What sound do you hear in *scuffle* that's missing in *scuff*? (/l/)
What sound do you hear in *slurp* that's missing in *slur*? (/p/)
What sound do you hear in *stain* that's missing in *sane*. (/t/)

**Initial Sound Deletion (Some Nonsense words)**
Say *locomotion* without the first sound. (ocomotion)
Say *jealous* without the first sound. (ealous)
Say *treasure* without the first sound. (rezure)
Say *thundercloud* without the first sound. (undercloud)

# Activity Forty-Seven*****

Warm-up

**Directions: Show the student the following three pictures.**

Ask: Look at the pictures. (wedding cake, typewriter, loafers)
-What two words have the same ending sound? (typewriter, loafer)
-How many syllables are in each word? (3, 3, 2)
-Reverse the first sounds in each word of *wedding cake.* (kedding wake)
-Reverse the syllables in *loafers.* (ersloaf)
-Reverse the first and last sounds in *loafers.* (zoaferl)
-Reverse the first and last sounds in *type.* (pyte)
-Say *typewriter* without the second syllable. (typer)
-Say *wedding cake* without the first sound in either word. (edding ake)
-Take the first syllable in *wedding cake* and the last syllable in *loafers.* (wedders)
-Take the first syllable in *loafers* and the second syllable in *wedding cake* and make a new word. (loafing)

Part II

**Pig Latin**
Say *feather* in Pig Latin. (eatherfay)
Say *pleasant* in Pig Latin. (leasantpay)
Say *sweatshirt* in Pig Latin. (weatshirtsay)
Say *tabloid* in Pig Latin. (abloidtay)
Say *newsboy* in Pig Latin. (ewsboynay)
Say *protein* in Pig Latin. (roteinpay)

**Vowel Substitution**
Say *galley*. Instead of /a/, say /o/. (golly)
Say *inscribe*. Instead of /i/, say /e/. (enscribe)
Say *casket*. Instead of /a/, say /u/. (cusket)

# Activity Forty-Eight*****

Warm-up

**Directions: Show the student the following three pictures.**

Ask: Look at the pictures. (piggy bank, trail mix, earrings)
-What word has a blend at the beginning? (trail mix-/tr/)
-How many syllables are in each word? (3, 2, 2)
-Reverse the first and last sounds in *piggy bank*. (kiggy banp)
-Reverse the words in *trail mix*. (mix trail)
-Reverse the words in *piggy bank*. (bank piggy)
-Say *piggy bank* without the second syllable. (pig bank)
-Take the first syllable in *piggy bank* and the last syllable in *trail mix* and make a new word. (pigmix)
-Take the first syllable in *trail mix*, the first syllable in *earrings*, and the last syllable in *piggy bank* and make a new word. (trail-ear-bank)

Part II

**Phoneme Switcheroo**
Reverse the first and last sounds in *symptom*. (mymptos)
Reverse the first and last sounds in *market*. (tarkem)
Reverse the first and last sounds in *directive*. (virectid)
Reverse the first and last sounds in *penance*. (senanp)
Reverse the first and last sounds in *caffeine*. (naffeik)
Reverse the first and last sounds in *perceive*. (verceip)

**Phoneme Generation**
Think of a word that has the same last sound as *restful*.
Think of a word that has the same last sound as *smooth*.
Think of a word that has the same final sound as *gruff*.
Think of a word that has the same final sound as *plenty*.

# Activity Forty-Nine*****

Warm-up

**Directions: Show the student the following three pictures.**

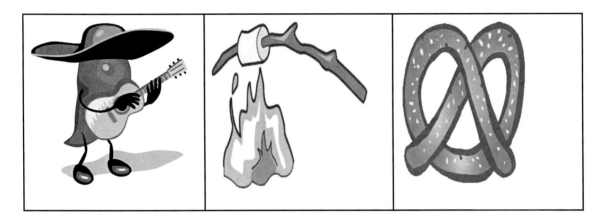

Ask: Look at the pictures. (chili pepper, marshmallow, pretzel)
-How many syllables are in each word? (4, 3, 2)
-What two words have a digraph in them? (chili pepper-/ch/, marshmallow-/sh/)
-What word begins with a blend? (pretzel-/pr/)
-Delete the last syllable in *chili pepper*. (chili pep)
-Reverse the first sounds in the words *chili pepper*. (pili chepper)
-Say *marshmallow* without the second syllable. (marsh-ow)
-Say *pretzel* without the first sound. (retzel)
-Take the first sound in *chili pepper* and the last syllable in *pretzel* and make a new word. (chilzel)
-Take the third syllable in *chili pepper*, the third syllable in *marshmallow,* and the last syllable in *pretzel* to make a new word. (pepowzel)

Part II

**Phoneme Switcheroo**
Reverse the first sounds in each syllable of *compete*. (pomkete)
Reverse the first sounds in each syllable in *forsake*. (sorfake)
Reverse the first sounds in each syllable in *frustrate*. (trusfrate)
Reverse the first sounds in each syllable in *headgear*. (geadhear)
Reverse the first sounds in each syllable in *threaten*. (treathen)
Reverse the first sounds in each syllable in *congress*. (goncress)

**Sound Deletion (some nonsense)**
Say *upswing* without the /w/. (upsing)
Say *entwine* without the /w/. (entine)
Say *gastric* without the /r/. (gastic)
Say *skinflint* without the /l/. (skinfint)

156

# Activity Fifty*****

Warm-up

**Directions: Show the student the following three pictures.**

Ask: Look at the pictures. (magnifier, combination lock, dancer)
-What two words have the same ending sound? (magnifier, dancer)
-How many syllables are in each word? (4, 5, 2)
-Say *magnifier* without the last syllable. (magnify)
-Say *dancer* without the last syllable. (dance)
-Reverse the words in *combination lock.* (lock combination)
-Delete the first syllable in *magnifier*. (ni-fier)
-Take the first syllable in *magnifier* and the second syllable in *combination lock* to make a new word. (magbin)
-Take the second syllable in *combination lock*, the second syllable in *magnifier* and the last syllable in *dancer* to make a new word. (binnifcer)

Part II

**Pig Latin**
Say *mistress* in Pig Latin. (istressmay)
Say *spinster* in Pig Latin. (pinstersay)
Say *nostril* in Pig Latin. (ostrilnay)
Say *pilgrim* in Pig Latin. (ilgrimpay)
Say *mushroom* in Pig Latin. (ushroommay)
Say *fabric* in Pig Latin. (abricfay)

**Phoneme Switcheroo**
Reverse the first and last sounds in *clap*. (plack)
Reverse the first and last sounds in *pinch*. (chinp)
Reverse the first and last sounds in *march*. (charm)

# *References*

Goldworthy, C. (1996). *Developmental Disabilities: A Language-Based Treatment Approach.* San Diego: Singular Publishing Group, Inc.

Goldworthy, C. (1998). *Sourcebook of Phonological Awareness Activities With Classic Children's Literature.* San Diego: Singular Publishing Group, Inc.

Henry, M. (2003) *Unlocking Literacy: Effective Decoding and Spelling Instruction.* Baltimore: Paul Brooks Publishing.